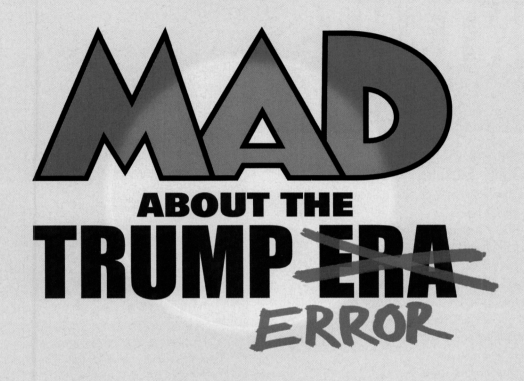

MAD
ABOUT THE
TRUMP ~~ERA~~ ERROR

**BY
"THE USUAL GANG OF IDIOTS"**

**EDITED BY
BILL MORRISON & DAN TELFER**

**MAD
BOOKS**

TABLE OF CONTENTS

@#$!

© 2019 by E.C. Publications, Inc. All Rights Reserved.
MAD and all related indicia are trademarks of E.C. Publications, Inc.
Published by MAD Books. An imprint of E.C. Publications, Inc., 2900 W. Alameda Ave., Burbank, CA 91505.

No part of this book may be reproduced in any form or by any electronic or mechanical means,
including information storage and retrieval systems, without permission in writing from the publisher,
except in the case of brief quotations embodied in critical articles and reviews.

The names and characters used in MAD fiction and semi-fiction are fictitious. A similarity without
satiric purpose to a living person is a coincidence.

Printed by Transcontinental Interglobe, Beauceville, QC, Canada. 8/23/19.
Second Printing.
Library of Congress Cataloging-in-Publication Data is available.
ISBN 978-1-4012-9346-8

Start using your smartphone for something dumb! MAD is available for mobile devices on Comixology,
Amazon Kindle, Magzter, and Google Play Newsstand (basically, everywhere except your weather app).

MARK FREDRICKSON COVER ARTIST

VERY FINE PEOPLE ON BOTH SIDES

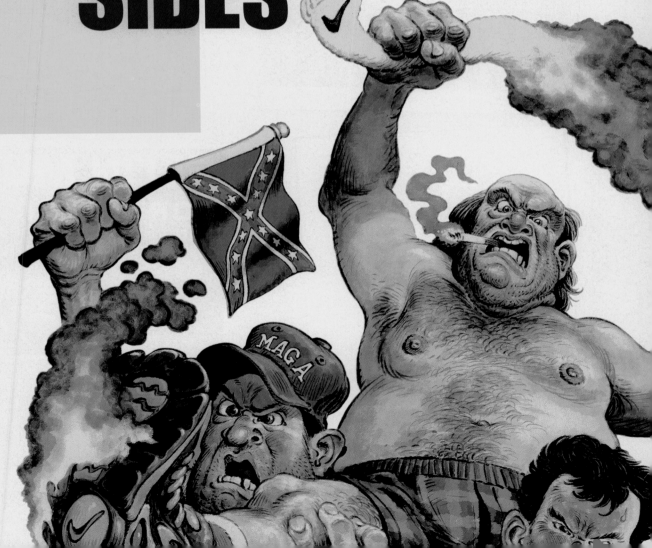

Oprah running for president? Sure, why not! Oprah's great. And her name is very easy to remember, which tests as the most important issue for the average American vote

CELEBRITY POLITICAL PO

(Paid for With Some Money Stedman Found in the Dryer)

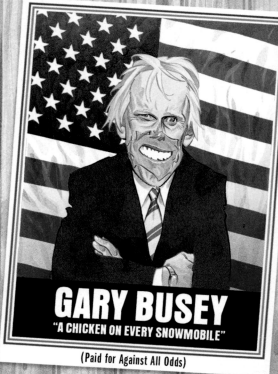

GARY BUSEY
"A CHICKEN ON EVERY SNOWMOBILE"
(Paid for Against All Odds)

GUY FIERI FOR PRESIDENT
FORMER MAYOR OF FLAVORTOWN
SORRY ABOUT THE DIARRHEA!

(Paid for by the Committee to Elect Robots From the Future)

WRITER **BLAINE CAPATCH**   ARTIST **ALEJANDRO RIVAS**

STERS WE'D LIKE TO SEE

J.K. Rowling '20

She Wasn't Born in America, But to Be Perfectly Honest, None of That Codswallop Really Matters Anymore, Now Does It?

(Paid for by Rowling, Who Made the Money Back in 15 Seconds)

gwyneth: a lifestyle president

★ ★ ★ ★ ★

A candidate unlike any other... delicately handpicked by constituents, bathed in Madagascar almond milk and consciously uncoupled from NRA donations, Gwyneth luxuriates the voter in artisanal detachment from the horrors of regular life.

Vote now and receive a free vaginal egg-dying kit for Easter.

Egg Size: S, M, L, XL, Ostrich

ADD TO VOTE   MAYBE LATER

(Paid for by the Three Rich Weirdos Who Actually Buy Things on Goop)

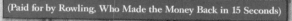

VOTE CLOONEY THOSE EYES!

(Paid for by the Committee to Elect George Clooney Before It's Possibly Revealed He Did Something Horrible)

Bawitdaba Da Bang Da Bang Diggy Diggy Diggy Shake the Boogie Said Up Jump the Presidency

MY NAME IS PREZ ROCK!

Corporations Are People, and This One Is Running for President

Pfizer 2020

Vote Pfizer or We'll Take Your Inhaler off the Market

VOTE 4 ALFRED!

ROSEANNE SHIFTS BLAME FOR RACIST RANT

BETTER LYING THROUGH CHEMISTRY

Roseanne Barr writes a racist tweet, loses her show, and blames it on Ambien. Come on, who blames outrageous behavior on a sleeping pill? Ridiculous...that's no excuse! But there is a new, even more culpable prescription drug!

WRITER
DICK DEBARTOLO

ARTIST
SCOTT ANDERSON

Introducing
the New Medical Breakthrough Pill:

Blame-ium

You take the drug, *it* takes the blame!

Just two tablets will loosen your tongue!*

*And probably your bowels, so make sure to have your small-minded meltdown near a restroom.

FORMER TV STAR ROSEANNE SAYS:

"I make **one** lousy 'racist' tweet and suddenly my show is cancelled, my co-stars hate me, and my career is over! And to top it off, I just found out there's a new drug I could have blamed it on! Where the eff you see kay was Blame-ium a few months ago when I needed it?"

GUARANTEED TO WORK!
If the **public** doesn't agree that your **tone-deaf** and **insensitive** words are the fault of **Blame-ium**, you get your **money back** (but not your reputation or TV show)!

LOSE WEIGHT, TOO!
Although **Blame-ium** is not a diet drug, many users **do** lose weight! A Blame-ium-induced rant often results in a punch in the mouth. Then eating must be done through a straw, and the pounds just melt away!

BLAME-IUM IS NOT FOR EVERYONE
While we'll **sell** it to everyone, it's probably not great for toddlers.

TALK TO YOUR DOCTOR
Better yet, talk to **our** doctor. Or, for complete **peace of mind**, don't talk to **any** doctor. Or, why not go to our website **www.blame-ium.con** and **print your own doctor diploma?** Then take as much **Blame-ium** as you damn well please!

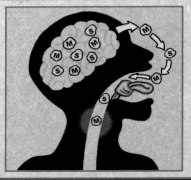

Your brain is made up of different types of cells, like **smart mouth cells** and **moronic mouth cells.** When you're inclined to say something stupid, the smart cells get knotted up with the moronic ones, leaving you tongue-tied and preventing jerk-wad comments. **Blame-ium** loosens those **knots** and sets your tongue free to say **any foul thing that comes into your head!** You're a **new person!** Often a person without a **job, family, or friends**...but still a **new person!** But now you have something to blame your idiocy on: **Blame-ium!**

COMING SOON:
ERASE-IUM!
Makes your mind a **total blank** so you won't remember **anything** you said or did. **Erase-ium** strips away another layer of personal accountability, allowing you to **deny with confidence,** even while hooked up to a lie detector!

Despite all the video and audio evidence, I don't recall saying "You also had some very fine people on both sides."

Hmm... checks out.

SIDE EFFECTS: Too numerous to fit in this ad, but basically everything short of **death**.
(Though **don't rule out death. And if you do pass away, don't blame us; we're all on Blame-ium, too!**)

Ever since Donald Trump was elected President, liberals have vowed to fight his every executive order, policy idea and moronic tweet — leading to protests, petitions and social-media howling. But as time has gone on, those bleeding hearts' idealism has begun to face up to the cold, orange facts of reality — as you'll see in this piece we call...

A Liberal HOPES / A Liberal KNOWS

A LIBERAL *HOPES*...
To spend all his free time protesting in an earnest effort to effect change

A LIBERAL *KNOWS*...
After a week or two, he'll spend all his free time binge-watching sitcoms on Netflix

A LIBERAL *HOPES*...
That Twitter will ban Trump, since his tweets could potentially pose a threat to national security

A LIBERAL *KNOWS*...
That they'll never ban Trump, since he's the only reason millions of users still bother with Twitter

WRITER: CHRISTIAN ALSIS   ARTIST: RICK TULKA   COLORIST: CARRIE STRACHAN

A LIBERAL *HOPES*...
To subscribe to *The New York Times* and *The Washington Post* to better support a free press

A LIBERAL *KNOWS*...
She'll go back to playing Candy Crush Saga on her tablet after hitting the *Times'* paywall

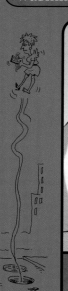

A LIBERAL *HOPES*...
To elevate the discourse by only debating issues of vital importance

A LIBERAL *KNOWS*...
That every political discussion she'll have will devolve into the mocking of Trump's hair, hands or golden-shower fetish

A LIBERAL *HOPES*...
To write to his Congressional Representatives, urging them to vote against repealing legislation like the Affordable Care Act

A LIBERAL *KNOWS*...
After three letters, he'll stop writing for fear of developing carpal tunnel syndrome and having it labeled a "preexisting condition"

A LIBERAL *HOPES...*
That protests will erupt at airports whenever Trump tries to enact a Muslim travel ban

A LIBERAL *KNOWS...*
That she'll change her tune the first time protest traffic causes her to miss her flight

A LIBERAL *HOPES...*
That a disastrous Trump presidency will cause history to look kindly upon the Obama administration

A LIBERAL *KNOWS...*
That even if Trump starts World War III with a deranged late-night tweet, half the country will somehow pin it on Obama

A LIBERAL *HOPES...*
That Democrats will find a transformative candidate who'll unite the masses in 2020

A LIBERAL *KNOWS...*
That they'll probably just trot out Hillary again

For a variety of reasons, there is a lot of protesting going on right now. Maybe you're one of the protestors — in which case, you need to make a sign! Or maybe you HATE protestors — in which case, the best way to let them know is by making a sign! Either way, we're here to help!

MAD'S TIPS FOR MAKING PROTEST SIGNS

If attending multiple protests, be sure to keep all your signs well-organized so you don't show up with the wrong one

Now is neither the time nor the place for your clever "promposals"

A sandwich board is a great way to get your message out, while keeping your hands free for eating sandwiches

Always, *always* spell-check

If you're going to use a famous quote, be aware that the ones you see on Facebook have a tendency to be misattributed

And lastly, don't forget to keep receipts of all your sign-making expenses. That way, George Soros can reimburse you later.

WRITER: KENNY KEIL   ARTIST: BOB STAAKE

"Right this way, sir! There's an Uber driver outside with a guide to all the local schools, theaters, concert venues, and churches!"

WRITER & ARTIST **LARS KENSETH**

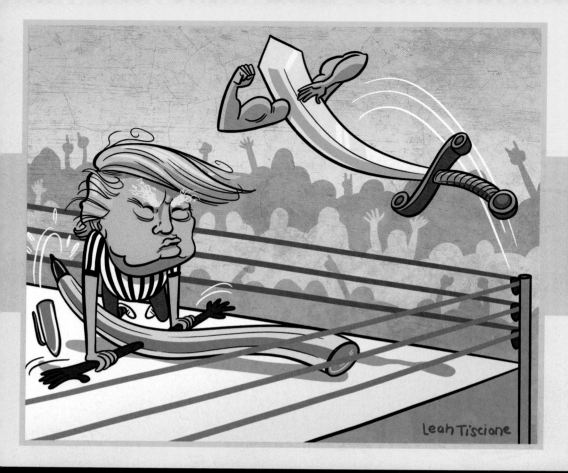

SEEN AT TRUMP'S RALLY IN MONTANA

WRITER **KIT LIVELY**
ARTIST **LEAH TISCIONE**

Leah Tiscione

MAKE HALLOWEEN GREAT AGAIN!
CANDIES FOR THE TRUMP ERA

WRITER & ARTIST **GIDEON KENDALL**

KU KLUX KISSES

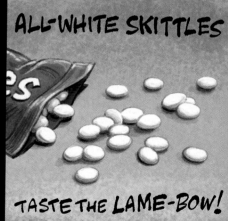

ALL-WHITE SKITTLES

TASTE THE LAME-BOW!

CLIMATE CHANGE IS A HOAX!

FINE PEOPLE ON BOTH SIDES

OBAMA IS A MUSLIM

PREZ CAN ABOLISH THE 14th AMENDMENT

DUMMIES

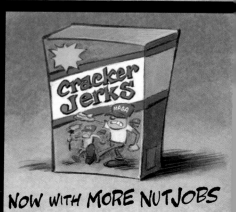

Cracker Jerks MAGA

NOW WITH MORE NUTJOBS

TRUMP BANS TRANSGENDER SOLDIERS
F. U. FOR YOUR SERVICE

Not long ago, President Trump boasted, "There's nobody bigger or better at the military than I am." Given his five sketchy deferments during the Vietnam War, exactly how he acquired his vast military knowledge is unclear. Maybe he watched a bunch of *M*A*S*H* reruns. In any event, in August, the ever-misguided Trump signed a directive banning transgender soldiers from military service. Secretary of Defense James Mattis, a retired general, was so horrified that he ordered a panel to look into the matter, thereby postponing the ban's implementation. Hopefully by the time Mattis' commission issues its report, Trump and Vice President Mike Pence—who reportedly wants to "hang" members of the LGBTQ community—will have been slapped with a ban on uninformed narcissists and holier-than-thou "Christians" from the White House.

I DON'T WANT YOU

NFL BLACKBALLS KAEPERNICK PERSONNEL FOUL

Colin Kaepernick began the 2017 NFL season as a former star quarterback in search of a job. But since he started taking a knee during the national anthem to protest unfair treatment of blacks, he was conspicuously ignored by all 32 NFL teams—including those in desperate need of a quarterback. Kaepernick's action suddenly became a referendum on whether you were a "real American": support him and it somehow followed that you don't support the troops—which makes as much sense as saying that if you don't support Kaepernick, you're a racist. With NFL ratings down, many attributed it to the widespread protests that Kaepernick inspired. On the other hand, maybe fans were disgusted by the collusion of rich white guys against one black man who had the temerity to exercise his Constitutional rights.

I **stand** here before you **today**, because whenever I **kneel**, some people have a **tendency** to lose their s#!t.

152 years after **Emancipation** we must face the tragic fact that the **black man** is still not treated **equally** in this country. That is why I began kneeling during the **national anthem.**

My **detractors**, including the **President**, have spread the **shallow lie** that I am protesting against the **flag** itself. I **honor** our **flag.** I **cherish** our **flag.** And so does the **NFL**, which only uses the **American flag** for solemn, respectful **pregame ceremonies**, as well as on the cheerleaders' skimpy titty tops.

Our great **flag** also appears on NFL-branded knit hats, T-shirts, decals, parking pass lanyards, red-white-and-blue footballs, rubber mouthpieces, monkey mittens, can coolers and 32 different "Stars and Stripes Tailgate Toss Games." That's what our brave military is fighting for! **God bless America!**

#STAY WOKE

DO THE RIGHT THING

WANT ADS

NFL RATINGS

WRITER: DESMOND DEVLIN   ARTIST: WARD SUTTON

I had a team.

I had a team…until I started protesting **systemic, unequal treatment.** And then the **NFL system** treated *me* unequally!

I had a team…but I was **dumped** for being a **distraction**... unlike the league's **hundreds of druggies, rapists, cheaters, child abusers, wife beaters** and **animal torturers.**

I had a team…the **San Francisco 49ers**, whose **roster** has had more **arrests** in the last **five years** than any other **team**, while the worst crime **I've** committed is hurting **Fox News'** feelings.

I had a team…in a **league** whose premiere franchise, the **New England Patriots**, is named after the **founding fathers** who stood up to their **government** in the spirit of **civic resistance** and carried out the **Boston Tea Party**, an act of **protest** which helped **forge** our nation's very **identity.** It's just a **good thing** they didn't **kneel!**

My friends, *I had a team*. And in the first **two months** I was off the **San Francisco 49ers** and completely **out of football,** I won the **same number of games** as the **entire 49ers team!**

I had a team, until I got **blackballed** by the **same** league that **now** publicly "**supports the players**" and preaches "**unity**" for everyone. Except me.

I had a team. But if the **courts** uphold my **legal grievance** over the **NFL's** flagrant **collusion** against me, I'll be **rich** enough to **own a team!**

Until then, though, my **schedule** is free, alas. **Free, alas!** I'm **VERY** available because I'm **free, alas!**

Unjustified **police shootings** must end. Only **then** will each of us be **judged NOT** by the **color** of our skin, but by the **content** of our **character**. But considering this **league** has **owners** who still stubbornly **defend** the ridiculous "**Redskins**" name, the **verdict is in** on the content of **their character!**

But I **say** to you this **day,** we are **not satisfied.** And we will **not be satisfied** until **justice** rolls down like **waters, and righteousness** like a **mighty stream.** But **until** that day **comes,** I **stand** before you here **today** to declare…

PROTESTERS BURNING NIKE PRODUCTS JUST DON'T IT

Education (or lack thereof) remains a major issue in the United States. Exhibit A: elementary schools seem to spend too much time on the three R's, and not nearly enough time on "don't light your clothes on fire." When Nike announced their partnership with peaceful protester/former NFL quarterback Colin Kaepernick in September, white nationalists took to their unkempt patios to incinerate their Nike apparel (which they'd already paid for). Nike's stock reached an all-time high just a week later, naturally. But not to worry, racists—your burnt offerings didn't go unnoticed here...

IDIOTS ON FIRE

This is the story of racist me[n]
who protest...not to protest..
but to waste a perfectl[y]
good pair of Air Jordans

They will sacrifice any Nik[e]
product to achieve their goals
Except their fitness tracker[s]

WRITER **CASEY BOYD** ARTIST **GIDEON KENDALL**

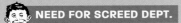

Trying to keep up with President Trump's relentless shenanigans is exhausting! And on top of that, then you also have to find the energy to complain about it! Who has the time? Luckily, MAD is stepping up in a yuge way and streamlining the whole process for you with our:

Make Your Own ANTI-TRUMP

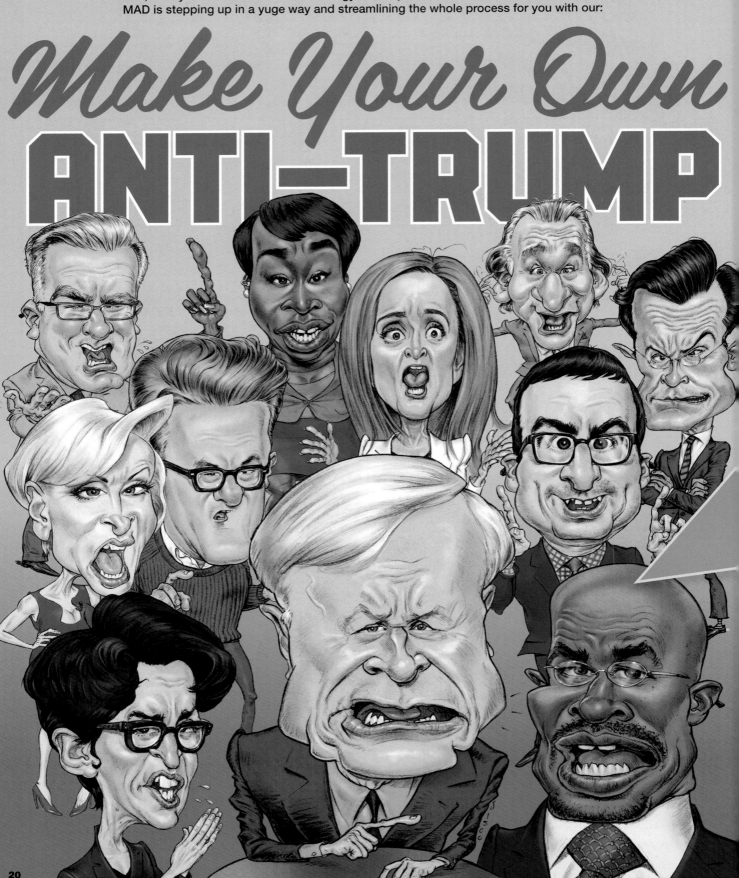

Someone tell me how a guy with a track record of _____

1) spreading racist conspiracy theories
2) misusing the phrase "on fleek"
3) texting interns the eggplant emoji
4) carving a penis into any table he sits at
5) leaving Melania steaming floaters
6) cheating at Pie Face with Barron

is our new President — even after he _____ !

1) talked about dating his hot daughter
2) coughed into his hand instead of his arm
3) stiffed that Times Square Elmo on a tip
4) vehemently defended Nickelback
5) snuck snacks from home into a movie theater
6) watched *This Is Us* completely out of order

RANT

WRITER: MATT LASSEN   ARTIST: SAM SISCO

Worse still, with absolutely ZERO facts, he still claims _____ !

1) there was widespread voter fraud
2) *Fuller House* is superior to the original
3) that his spicy guacamole is homemade and not store-bought
4) gravity is just a theory
5) the *Gremlins* movies are documentaries
6) Obama rigged his lottery scratch-offs

And to think he appointed _____

1) Steve Bannon
2) The "Flex Seal" Guy
3) Amazon's Alexa
4) Billy Bush
5) The former Verizon guy, now the Sprint guy
6) Dick Cheney's podiatrist

to be _____ !

1) his top advisor
2) *People*'s Sexiest Man Alive
3) Daniel Craig's replacement as James Bond
4) the new spokesman for Dollar Shave Club
5) the Clooneys' birthing coach
6) James Corden's new bandleader

If we don't do something, we can say goodbye to _____

1) basic human rights
2) quality Amish woodwork
3) any hope of reading a new *Game of Thrones* book anytime soon
4) those little wooden spoons you get with Italian ices
5) any chance of a *Westworld* porn parody happening
6) a *Paul Blart* Broadway musical

and prepare for four years of _____ !

1) praying Mike Pence doesn't become President
2) lingering Olympic fever
3) lackluster Kevin Hart vehicles
4) jokes involving the word "bigly"
5) disdain for cargo shorts
6) increasingly-confusing Oreo variations

I'm definitely going to the protest at _____ and

1) Trump Tower
2) the last remaining Radio Shack
3) a Redbox kiosk
4) participating Red Lobster locations
5) the site of the Bowling Green massacre
6) the Comedy Central roast of Brent Spiner

everyone there is going to _____ !

1) wear a pink pussy hat
2) eat cronuts like it's going out of style
3) massage each others' feet
4) receive a participation award
5) talk like a pirate
6) quietly mourn the death of Vine

EVERYTHING'S GONNA BE ALT-RIGHT DEPT.

NOT-TOO-BRIGHTBART

BIG GUMMINT   BIG FAKE NEWS   BIG LEFT–LEANING CORRUPT DEPRAVED HOLLYWOOD

NOT–TOO–BRIGHTBART WHITESVILLE | NOT–TOO–BRIGHTBART HATESTOWN | NOT–TOO–BRIGHTBART DEMAGOGUE ISLANDS | NOT–TOO–BRIGHTBART TEXAS

THE OFFICIAL NOT–TOO–BRIGHTBART STORE   FREE SHIPPING ON STEVE BANNON CASUAL WEAR

HOME   SUBSCRIBE

SHOP NOW >

SEARCH

WHATEVER IT TAKES TO FEED PARANOIA AND DENY SCIENCE WITH CURT SCHILLING
9–11AM EASTERN MONDAY–FRIDAY

MOST VICIOUS COMMENT-INDUCING

Publicly Funded Aquarium Allows Starfish to Change Gender
20,325 comments - 2 minutes ago

Army Vet Told To Leave Burning Restaurant
16,313 comments - 5 minutes ago

Sec'y of Defense Mattis Approves of Washboarding in Jug Bands
10,243 comments - 8 minutes ago

Mounting Evidence Suggests Soros May Be Palindromic
8,448 comments - 11 minutes ago

MUSLIM 'STAR WARS' COSPLAYERS AT CHICAGO COMIC-CON ALLEGEDLY USING SHARIA FORCE
by BEN SPEW
 1287

MARRIED MAN BANGING HOOKER IN CHEAP MOTEL DISGUSTED BY ABSENCE OF GIDEON BIBLE IN BEDSIDE TABLE: 'A FURTHER SIGN OF OUR CRUMBLING MORALITY'
by CHARLIE GNASH
 1580

9TH GRADE STUDENTS IN OHIO LANGUAGE CLASS FORCED TO LEARN FROM TEXTBOOKS PRINTED ENTIRELY IN SPANISH
by LUCAS NOSEBLEED
 1090

LEFTISTS PROTEST OPEN-CARRY TRAMPOLINE PARK
by JOEL B. PLAGUE
 289

REPORT: HILLARY ROLLS DOUBLES THREE TIMES PLAYING MONOPOLY; SOMEHOW AVOIDS JAIL
by SEAN MORASS
526

FINALLY! WHITE HOUSE UNVEILS TIMETABLE FOR PLANS TO STIR UP SOME SERIOUS SH*T WITH NORTH KOREA

Trump's schedule to include tweets to be sent from toilet at 4 AM and include references to Kim Jong-un as "a fat little loser, just a total loser."

by IAN HATCHET-BRAIN   3108

TRENDING NOW

Sponsored Links

You Won't Believe What TV's Fred Mertz Looks Like Today
Daily Exhumer

YOU MIGHT LIKE

TRUMP CALLS PUTIN'S PRIVATE CELL PHONE DIRECTLY TO ASK ABOUT CLINTONS' RUSSIAN TIES

ILLEGAL ALIENS GET TEMPORARY REPRIEVE AS TRUMP FOCUSES ON DEPORTING CELEBS WHO SAID THEY'D LEAVE IF HE WAS ELECTED **474**

CHUCK SCHUMER APPROVAL RATING UNFAIRLY SKEWS HIGHER DUE TO RESEMBLANCE TO BELOVED MR. HOOPER FROM 'SESAME STREET' **263**

CHRISTIAN-OWNED BAKERY TRICKED INTO MAKING WEDDING CAKE FOR GAY COUPLE WITH ANDROGYNOUS NAMES **160**

OPINION: WE CAN HOLD THE ISRAELI ARMY IN HIGH ESTEEM AND STILL NOT WANT ANY JEWS IN OUR NEIGHBORHOOD

BREAKING: IVANKA TRUMP FASHION LINE NOT AVAILABLE ON DULUTH TRADING CO. WEBSITE **443**

85

With Milo Gone From The Site, We No Longer Have To Pretend To Tolerate Homosexuals **201**

COULTER

Ann Coulter: No Matter What Trump Does Wrong, I'll Compare It Illogically To Something Obama Did **594**

HERE'S AN UNFLATTERING PHOTO OF MICHAEL MOORE IN RETALIATION FOR ALL THOSE HIDEOUS SHOTS OF STEVE BANNON THAT HUFFPO LIKES TO RUN

by RWA SQUAWKINS **663**

STUDY: DUMBOCRAT SJW SNOWFLAKES 'OFFENDED' BY TERM 'LIBTARD'

by CRASS W. STRUT **384**

WRITER: SCOTT MAIKO

ARTIST (TRUMP, SCHILLING, MELON BALLER): MIKE LOEW

You can't shield your children from the realities of the world forever, no matter how high you build that ~~wall~~ fence! So, on the off nights when you're not reading about engines that could, we recommend easing your little ones into modern misery with these...

Bedtime Stories
for the Trump Era

Big Girl Pants: Sucking it up and Learning to Tolerate Sexual Harassment

Lisa Has Two Daddies AND We Don't Have to Bake Them a Cake

Grandma Can't Come to Visit This Year

Maya Goes to Mexico!

DOIN' TIME! a Learn to Count Book

1 DIME BAG + 2 COPS + 1 OVER-ZEALOUS JUDGE = 10 YEARS in prison!

You Can't Go to the Doctor Unless You're Rich

Uery Fine People

Farewell, Polar Bears!

WRITER & ARTIST **NOMI KANE**

Whether you're just a casual xenophobe or the proud member of a recognized hate group, it's a great time to be a racist in America! After a white supremacist drove into a crowd of counter-protestors at August's "Unite the Right" rally in Charlottesville, Virginia—killing one and injuring 19—President Trump somehow couldn't manage to condemn Nazis (freakin' NAZIS!). But he DID manage to compliment some "very fine people" in the movement and blame "both sides" for the violence. President Sociopath even found time to speak out against the removal of Confederate statues, saying, "They're trying to take away our culture" (and who would know better than Trump, a third-generation immigrant from Queens?). We don't understand how defending racism helps to "make America great again"—but what do we know? We didn't understand "covfefe" either—and that was one of the more intelligent things Trump said all year.

JUSTICE KENNEDY HAS ANNOUNCED HIS RETIREMENT FROM THE SUPREME COURT.

AS A RESULT, MASLOW HAS UPDATED HIS HIERARCHY OF NEEDS:

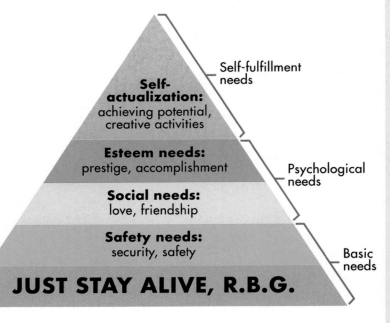

Self-fulfillment needs

Self-actualization: achieving potential, creative activities

Esteem needs: prestige, accomplishment

Psychological needs

Social needs: love, friendship

Safety needs: security, safety

Basic needs

JUST STAY ALIVE, R.B.G.

WRITER **RIANE KONC**

I REALLY DON'T CARE, DO U?

JUSTICE KENNEDY ANNOUNCES HIS RETIREMENT

ARTIST **IVAN EHLERS**

WE FLIP HOUSES
1-555-DEM-OCRATS

SNOWFLAKES ROASTING ON AN OPEN FIRE

you smell burning, it's because comedian Michelle Wolf **roasted** the GOP at this year's White House Correspondents' Dinner. You would think the party with elephant mascot would have thicker skin, but they got redder in the face than Sarah Huckabee Sanders' perfected bold lip. SNL alum and obscure-reference conteur Dennis Miller came to their rescue by promising to retaliate with brutally mean jokes about the scariest 'wolf' since Virginia in **three days** flat. Not e most impressive turnaround, but since when is **timing** important to comedy? Sadly, Miller's burns never materialized, leaving the poor GOP waiting like adimir and Estragon for Godot, babe!

Michelle WOLF

Dennis MILLER

Ha-ha vs. Cha-Cha!

Who's Afraid to Write Jokes About MICHELLE WOLF?

he Made Fools of the GOP!
They Were Outraged!
But He'll Get Her Back...
IN THREE DAYS!

2

THE BEST PEOPLE

SEAN SPICER, WHITE HOUSE PRESS SECRETARY
SPINNER AND LOSER

What happens when you add a few grains of truth to a steaming pot of lies, obfuscation and amateurish numbskullery? You get White House Press Secretary Sean Spicer's 2017 press conferences, which reached operatic levels of toxicity as he insisted (among dozens of other whoppers) that Trump's inaugural crowd was the biggest ever, millions voted illegally in the Presidential election and Adolf Hitler was a decent guy. But he was so bad at serving up Trump's foul stew of mendacity that he was dumped in July for the even sourer Sarah Huckabee Sanders—leaving behind little more than the memory of an irritating toady and a bitter aftertaste.

Cooking up a lie without the right ingredients?
That's a recipe for disaster!

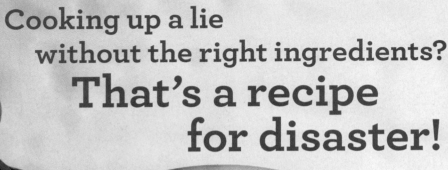

PAUL MANAFORT FLIPS FRAUDIAN SLIP

Sleazeball Russian lobbyist and former Trump campaign manager Paul Manafort would've gotten away with stealing millions and cheating the IRS, but he made one fatal mistake: he helped get Trump elected and landed on the radar of the special counsel investigation! Paulie Walnuts may not pay his taxes, but he kept EXCELLENT financial records. And after being convicted of eight counts of fraud, he flipped to the side of Robert Mueller, who squeezes this battle royale like a certain swarming purple storm in a popular video game. Maybe Manafort will ride the storm and glide away, but regardless, Mueller's power button is controlling Manafort now.

MANAFORTNITE

NOW AVAILABLE FOR DOWNLOAD
ON BURNER PHONES AND CONSOLES PURCHASED WITH LAUNDERED MONEY!

15,000

CYPRUS ACCOUNT BANKBOOK

TREASON

T

PERJURY TRAP

PRESIDENTIAL PARDON

PLAY FOR FREE!
(all in-app purchases will be charged to taxpayers)

CONTENT RATED BY
ESRB

WRITER **DESMOND DEVLIN**   ARTIST **DEAN MACADAM**

JEFF SESSIONS' BORDER BOOK

WRITER & ARTIST **LUKE MCGARRY**

2017 was the year in which conspiracy theories went mainstream—when millions of ignoramus Americans could comfortably revel in and defend their non-fact-based beliefs. And nobody (with the possible exception of President Trump) embodied or promoted such monstrous falsehoods more flagrantly than Alex Jones, the deranged *Infowars* host who, sadly, now stands at the vanguard of poisonous online mouth-breathers. Although his gullible flock now sees him as an old-fashioned hero, fearlessly speaking truth to power at every turn, our dearest wish is for a giant boulder to roll down from above and squash him like the bug he is.

INFOWARS JONES
and the
BABBLE of
CONSPIRACIES

HILLARY HEADS A CHILD PORNO RING!

9/11 WAS AN INSIDE JOB!

SANDY HOOK WAS A HOAX!

OBAMA CREATED ISIS!

POLICE LINE DO NOT CROSS

ARTIST: MARK STUTZMAN

The Fast Five
WAYS NEIL GORSUCH CELEBRATED HIS SUPREME COURT APPOINTMENT

1 Sent thank-you flowers to his mentor, Judge Judy

2 Urged his friends to get abortions now, before he makes them illegal

3 Sent prank job listings to Merrick Garland

4 Brushed up on the Constitution, so that he can better misinterpret it

5 Joined Samuel Alito in a spirited game of "Gavel Keep-away" from Ruth Bader Ginsburg

Artist: Anton Emdin

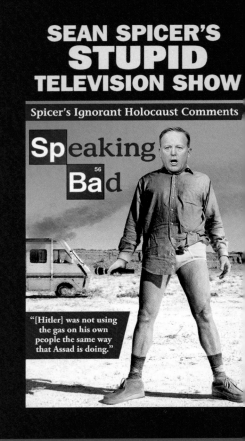
THE ROAD TO JUSTICE (HOPEFULLY)

WRITER **TAMMY GOLDEN**
ARTIST **LEAH TISCIONE**

SARAH HUCKABEE SANDERS HER GIG MAKES US GAG

It's no secret that the current administration is a joke, and one of the main players in this felonious farce is press secretary Sarah Huckabee Sanders. With an unblinking ability to twist the truth like a balloon animal and a monotone delivery that rivals Steven Wright, Huckabee Sanders has perfected working the main room of the White House. Handling hecklers with a rapid-fire, honed delivery of lies and deliberately confusing rhetoric, she shows time and time again that she owns the stage. But fame is fleeting, and we can only hope that it won't be long before the spotlight leaves her behind.

Imploding lives using hearsay
Immoral lady undoes history
Infuriate liberals using hogwash
Instantly legitimizes unpleasant hicks
I literally understand Hell

i'm lying up here

treason premiere
MON · FRI or when we feel like it SHILTIME

WRITER **KIT LIVELY**   ARTIST **MIKE LOEW**

JOINT U.S.-NORTH KOREA SUMMIT AGREEMENT

Supreme Leader Kim Jong Un and Unparalleled President Donald J. Trump have agreed to the following ideas, notions, and concepts, set forth on this day, the 12th of June, Two Thousand Eighteen. No take-backs, double-dog dares, or calling infinity.

- North Korea will agree to "not be so obvious" in their lies about discontinuing their nuclear program.

- Both countries agree that kimchi is a tasty addition to any meal.

- Each leader agrees to refrain from commenting on the other's hair.

- Immediately following their negotiations, the leaders will make a cool fort out of all those flags.

- Both countries agree that dogs shall no longer be allowed to play basketball.

- Donald Trump agrees to replace the U.S.-South Korea joint military exercises with an annual game of Battleship, to which South Korean President Moon Jae-in will not be invited.

- Both the U.S. and North Korea agree that this document has no teeth and in no way binds or obligates either party.

Donald J. Trump
President of the United States

Kim Jong Un
Supreme Leader of North Korea

Witnessed by
Dennis Rodman

Celebrate the only effective statement out of the Oval Office since Trump trundled into the presidency: Melania's fashion! Our occasional First Lady of the White House has made her mark on hearts across the nation with her poise, compassion, and **pretty clothes!** Our sartorial stylist Sina Grace predicts what inspired looks Melania will wear in 2019 to do her part in making America look great again!

MELANIA TRUMP PAPER DOLL

Blunderingly Purchased MAGA Cap — MAKE AMERICA GAY AGAIN

Oversize Statement Chapeau — ALSO AVAILABLE IN **BLACK**

Avant-Garde Face Mask

Kute Kim Kover-Up

Designer Slogan Shades — BE BEST

Cute Flag Ascot

Flirty Jersey — Draft Dodger's Wife

Golden Handcuffs

Highly Embellished Cut-Offs

Staffs Are In *MADE IN CHINA

Versatile Bag that Works for Hub's Breakfast, Lunch, or Dinner

Post-Op Recovery Outfit

High Heels for Wearing to Disaster Sites

Book Club Selects for Quick Golf Weekends at Mar-a-Lago — FRECKLES NOT FECKLESS

WRITER & ARTIST **SINA GRACE**

TED CRUZ STANDS UP TO TRUMP

WRITER & ARTIST **LARS KENSETH**

"Children shouldn't be taken from their parents. Here are some other tough stances I've taken. Murder: not cool. Hitler: just the worst. Ice cream: tasty…"

The Stupider Six
SURPRISES IN IVANKA TRUMP'S BOOK

1 She mistakenly thinks she's third in line to the Presidency

2 Her first word as a baby? "Bankruptcy"

3 Many of the book's "inspirational quotes" attributed to famous women are actually old Pepsi slogans

4 Even *she* voted for Hillary

5 She only started dating Jared Kushner because she thought he was the guy from the Subway ads

6 Ivanka feels so strongly about opportunities for women, she insisted on a female ghostwriter

WRITER **JEFF KRUSE**
ARTIST **ED STECKLEY**

TRUMP VS. KIM JONG-UN ATOM & EVE OF DESTRUCTION

We hope you're reading this. It's an iffy proposition because, as we go to press, President Trump and North Korea's Kim Jong-un seem uncomfortably close to launching a nuclear war. If that happens and you're in the strike zone, you'll be incinerated faster than a marshmallow being held over a roaring campfire by a two-year-old—not good news for you and millions of others (or for MAD, since we can't afford to lose too many more readers and stay in business)! We wish we could be more optimistic, but given the North Korean dictator's unstable past, and Trump taunting him as "Little Rocket Man," we wouldn't blame you if you put this issue down now and started digging a bunker in your basement.

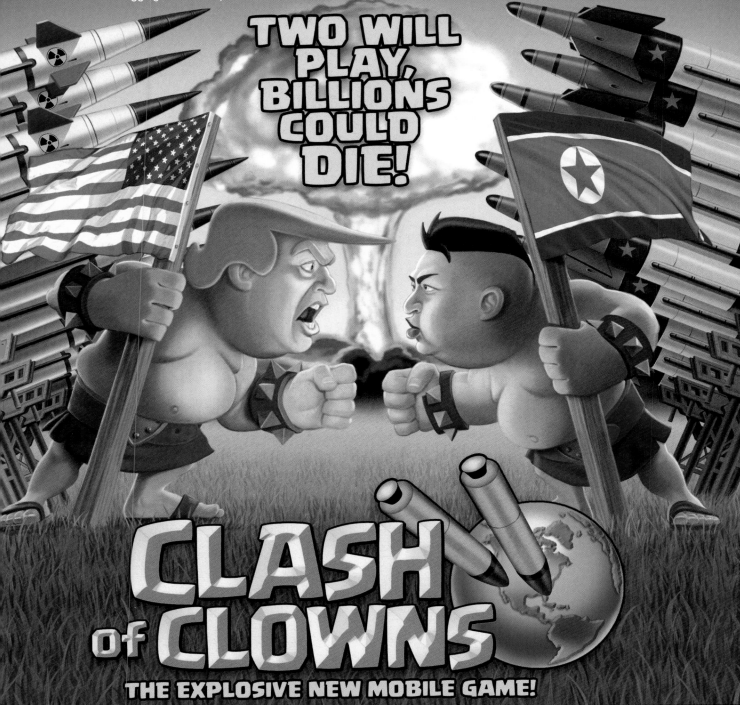

TWO WILL PLAY, BILLIONS COULD DIE!

CLASH of CLOWNS
THE EXPLOSIVE NEW MOBILE GAME!

Use your resources: irresponsible threats, a disconnect from reality and, of course, nuclear missiles to lead your village into its greatest – and final – battle!

Play as either a power-hungry, child-like dictator or an immature, influence-craving despot! The choice is yours!

Wipe your opponents off the planet before they do the same to you, mere moments later. The last team to perish in a nuclear holocaust (briefly) wins!

CLASH of CLOWNS

AVAILABLE (FOR NOW) ON iOS AND ANDROID

The Blue Spokes-Boy
by Alejandro Rivas, after Thomas Gainsborough

Girl with the Really
Expensive Line of Earrings
by Roberto Parada, after Johannes Vermeer

THE
MADROPOLITAN

ARTISTS   **ALEJANDRO RIVAS   ROBERTO PARADA   MARK STUTZMAN   JAMES WARHOLA**

Arrangement in Gold and Black No. 1
(Barron's Mother)
by Mark Stutzman, after James A. McNeill Whistler

Kellyanne: Dancing Around the Truth
by James Warhola, after Edgar Degas

MUSEUM OF ART
THE TRUMP COLLECTION

The Stupid Six
CHANGES BEING MADE TO WHITE HOUSE PRESS BRIEFINGS

1 Each briefing will begin with the Trump Loyalty Oath

2 Sean Spicer will soon have a "Phone a Friend" option

3 Correspondents will be barred from reporting on anything said at briefings

4 Sarah Huckabee Sanders will now be doing 50% of the lying and misleading

5 Reporters will be discouraged from making hand-jerking motions after Spicer speaks

6 Correspondents from CNN, *The New York Times* and *The Washington Post* will receive special "Fake News Credentials."

Artist: Tom Richmond

"Mike Pence is no more, Mother. There is only Lodestar."

WRITER & ARTIST **LARS KENSETH**

PEARLS OF WISDOM A YOUNG TRUMP MAY HAVE OVERHEARD

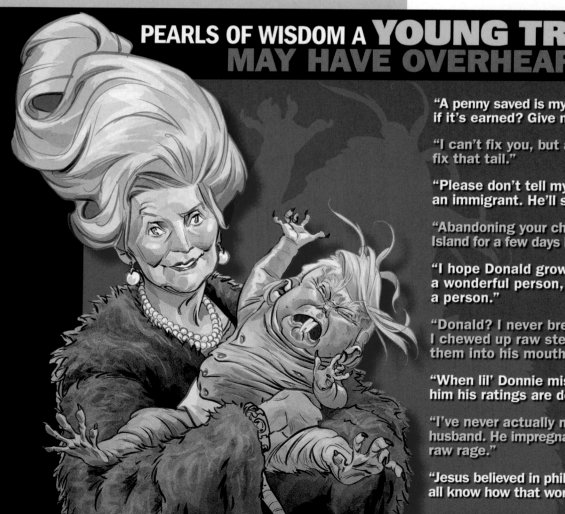

"A penny saved is my penny. Who cares if it's earned? Give me your penny."

"I can't fix you, but a doctor can fix that tail."

"Please don't tell my son that I'm an immigrant. He'll start shrieking."

"Abandoning your children at Coney Island for a few days builds character."

"I hope Donald grows up to be a wonderful person, or at least a person."

"Donald? I never breastfed him. I chewed up raw steaks and spit them into his mouth."

"When lil' Donnie misbehaves, I tell him his ratings are down."

"I've never actually made love to my husband. He impregnated me with his raw rage."

"Jesus believed in philanthropy, and we all know how that worked out for him."

WRITER **DAN TELFER**   ARTIST **ALEJANDRO RIVAS**

MIKE PENCE WON'T DINE ALONE WITH A WOMAN
AND EAT US NOT INTO TEMPTATION

Vice President Mike Pence has an eating disorder. No, it's not anorexia, bulimia or posting pictures of every damn thing he eats on Instagram. His problem is refusing to eat with a woman who isn't his wife. Why? Maybe Pence thinks he's such a hunk that women won't be able to keep their hands off him. Or maybe he fears that he won't be able to keep *his* devilish hands off *them*—or because when he was governor of Indiana, he enacted a handful of draconian reproductive-rights laws and he doesn't want to get an earful about what an a**wipe he is. Whatever the reason, if you're female and have business to attend to with the veep, pack a lunch— because to Mike Pence, dining alone with a female is his Kryptonite.

WRITER:
JEFF KRUSE

ARTIST:
R. SIKORYAK

*"Rudy, I just want to thank you and your team
for all the great work you're doing!"*

WRITER & ARTIST **LARS KENSETH**

"MITCH MCCONNELL HAD A JOB"
(SUNG TO THE TUNE OF "OLD MACDONALD HAD A FARM")

Mitch McConnell had a job
*He **re-fused** to **do**;*
*Would **not** vote on **Obama's** judge*
*He just said "**F-you!**"*
*With a **no-no** here*
*And a **no-no** there,*
*Here a **no**, there a **no***
***Garland** is a "**no-go**,"*
Mitch McConnell** had a **job
*He **refused** to **do***

*Mitch McConnell changed his **mind***
*With **Trump's nom-in-ee**;*
*He said the **Senate** had to **vote***
*Such **hypocrisy!***
*With an **aye-aye** here*
*And an **aye-aye** there,*
*Here an **aye**, there an **aye***
***Gorsuch** is a "**great guy**,"*
Mitch McConnell** changed his **mind
*With **Trump's nom-in-ee***

Artist: Ward Sutton

WHICH OF TRUMP'S PICKS DO YOU THINK WILL BE THE NEXT SUPREME COURT JUSTICE?

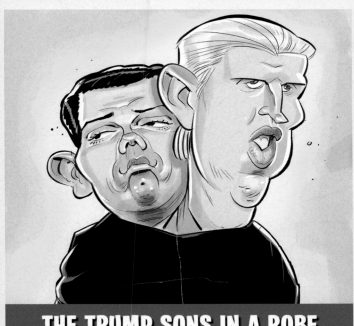

THE TRUMP SONS IN A ROBE

THE GHOST OF PHYLLIS SCHLAFLY

JUDGE REINHOLD

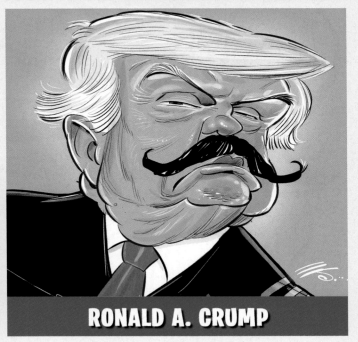

RONALD A. CRUMP

ARTIST **ED STECKLEY**

ONE HOLDOUT JUROR
IN THE MANAFORT TRIAL REVEALED

WRITER & ARTIST IVAN EHLERS

BRETT KAVANAUGH'S SUPREME COURT HEARINGS
INNOCENT UNTIL PROVEN RIDICULOUS

Things were going all right as the Senate Judiciary Committee was conducting their hearings to confirm the next Supreme Court justice, until word got out that Dr. Christine Blasey Ford had accused the maybe-not-so-Honorable Judge Brett Kavanaugh of sexually assaulting her one summer when they were both in high school, a charge he aggressively (and with spittle) denied. But luckily, Brett possessed just the doodled documents he needed to prove where he *wasn't* that season: his 1982 calendar! Sure enough, amid his sporting events, workouts, and movies, there is not one single entry for being wasted, pinning a girl down, and grinding on her while muffling her screams! Thank golly he had this evidence, or else we could've ended up with some scattered Supreme Court justice who doesn't keep such pristine records of what he didn't do!

NEW for 2019!
The Honorable Justice Brett Kavanaugh's
ALIBI-A-DAY Desk Calendar!

That's right, 365 days of innocence are yours in this handy tabletop calendar, with easy to read whereabouts for every day of the year! Your future will be conviction-free with this attractive tabletop calendar that has you scheduled for week after week of non-criminal activities!

Now there's **no excuse** not to have a **good excuse**, *so order yours today!*

JUDGE BRETT KAVANAUGH
★★★ ALIBI-A-DAY ★★★
2019 DESK CALENDAR

PRINTED ON HI-QUALITY HARD STOCK THAT WILL HOLD UP TO SCRUTINY & LAST FOR DECADES!

★★★ PUBLISHED BY WHITE PRIVILEGE PRESS ★★★

MADE IN THE SHADE

ONLY $19.82

WRITER & ARTIST TERESA BURNS PARKHURST

DECEMBER 10
tried to convince Ashley, AGAIN, that "boof" means fart

SEPTEMBER 20
was super impartial for a few hours

JANUARY 6
lunch with Clarence T. at Hooters

MAY 28
treated several women very appropriately

MARCH 17
tried all day to get Bader Ginsburg to like me

ALSO AVAILABLE:
Beer-at-a-Glance Wall Calendar!

OCTOBER 5
reordered fruit of the month subscription for Sue Collins (thanks again!)

CHECK OUT:
The Judge's
I Didn't Plan It, DID YOU?
Daily Planner!

Order today and we'll include a FREE tote for handy carrying to and from testimony!

FLOTUS VISITS CAPTURED KIDS ON THE BORDER

DISPASSION FAUX PAS

First Lady Melania Trump has done her share of dumb things this year, from launching her "Be Best" campaign with information and graphics plagiarized from an Obama-era pamphlet, to getting busted by her hubby for watching "fake news" on CNN at 45,000 feet on Air Force One. But the gaffe that garnered the most attention occurred as she left Washington for McAllen, Texas, to visit a shelter for immigrant children U.S. Border Patrol had separated from their parents. The First Lady sported a jacket with the message "I REALLY DON'T CARE, DO U?" printed in large letters on the back. Was this commentary on her feelings for the plight of traumatized kids, or a thoughtless fashion choice? Either way, this story of biblically dumb proportions reminds us of another notorious coat that got its wearer into trouble...

"Vastly more clueless than
Off-Broadway's *Clueless: The Musical*"
–New Yecch Times

MELANIA AND THE AMAZING TONE-DEAF GREEN COAT

NEDAMIRROR THEATER
1600 Pennsylvania Ave., Washington, D.C.

WRITER & ARTIST **R. WILCOX DECKERT**

"*Okay, Mike Pence and silhouettes of all the people I've fired, let's get to work!*"

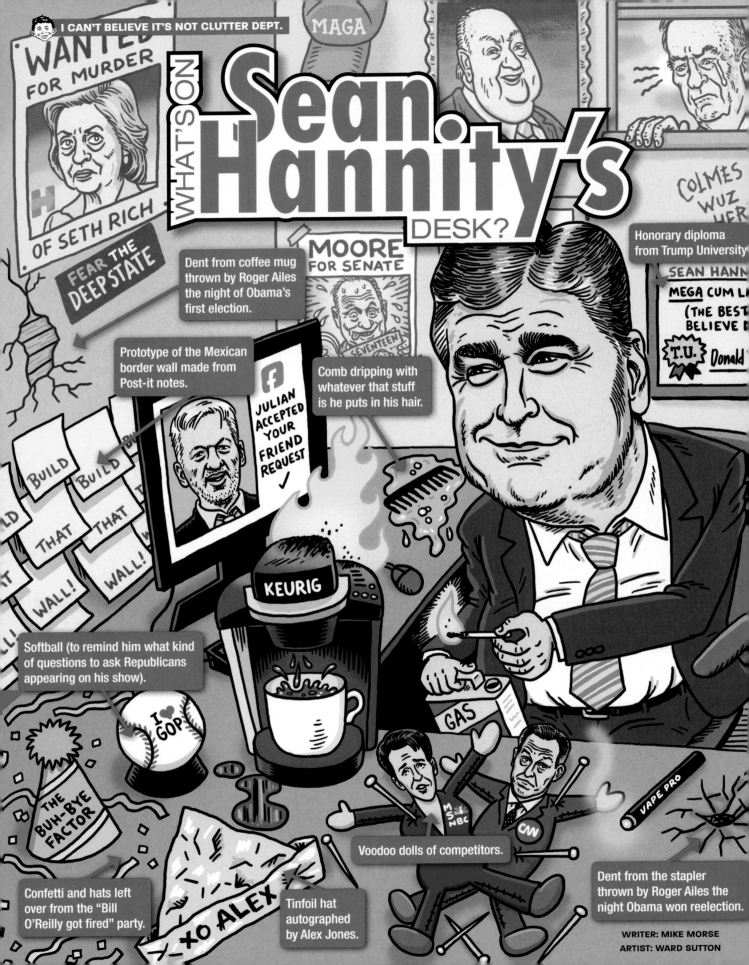

Yeah, I'm not sure how either of us got here.

WHITE HOUSE CORRUPTION DREDGE OF ALLEGIANCE

An EPA chief who denies climate change? Check! A frack-happy Secretary of the Interior who loves big-game trophy hunting? Check and check! A gaggle of inner-circle bozos burning jet fuel for personal jaunts? We hear Moscow is beautiful this time of year! And yet none of them can hold a candle to the king: Donald Trump has reportedly spent nearly $80 million of U.S. taxpayer money on golf trips since taking office. Which has us thinking...

WRITER & ARTIST **LUKE MCGARRY**

WRITER **KIT LIVELY** ARTIST **LEAH TISCIONE**

"In the future, an American president will criticize Germany for not spending enough on its military."

WRITER & ARTIST **LARS KENSETH**

Melania Is Finally Spotted

WRITER & ARTIST **BOB ECKSTEIN**

HOW DOES DONALD TRUMP JR. STACK UP AGAINST OTHER FAMOUS JUNIORS?

ALE EARNHARDT JR.
Has twice won the Daytona 500

DONALD TRUMP JR.
Thanks to chauffeurs, doesn't know how to drive

WINNER: EARNHARDT!

KEN GRIFFEY JR.
Was called "The Kid"

DONALD TRUMP JR.
Is called "That a**hole's kid"

WINNER: GRIFFEY!

FLOYD MAYWEATHER JR.
Went toe-to-toe with Conor McGregor

DONALD TRUMP JR.
Got into a Twitter spat with Chelsea Handler

WINNER: MAYWEATHER!

CAL RIPKEN JR.
Holds the record for consecutive games played

DONALD TRUMP JR.
Never worked a day in his life

WINNER: RIPKEN!

JUNIOR MINTS
Coated in a layer of delicious milk chocolate

DONALD TRUMP JR.
Coated in a thin sheen of rich-brat sweat and arrogance

WINNER: MINTS!

MARTIN LUTHER KING JR.
Orated the immortal words, "I have a dream"

DONALD TRUMP JR.
Emailed the incriminating words, "If it's what you say I love it"

WINNER: KING!

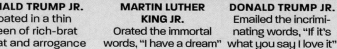

55

The Note Trump Left in Israel's Western Wall

DEAR GOD,

PLEASE CONTACT ME WITH THE NAME OF THE CONTRACTOR WHO BUILT THIS WALL.

I HAVE A SIMILAR PROJECT AND WOULD LIKE A QUOTE.

-DJT

MIKE PENCE'S JOKE CORNER

Here are some of the favorite jokes of a man who is not boring, bland or creepy, and who enjoys hilarious humor.

 Knock-knock.

Who's there?

Mike Pence.

Q: What has two thumbs and is the Vice President?

A: Me, Vice President Mike Pence.

Q: What's black and white and red all over?

A: A newspaper. The humor of this joke comes from how "read" – as in "having read a newspaper" – sounds the same as "red," the color.

WRITER **BRIAN BOONE**   ARTIST **CHRIS HOUGHTON**

THE CURRENT STATE OF NUCLEAR TALKS

WITH APOLOGIES TO SPARKY

HERE WE GO WITH ANOTHER RIDICULOUS
MAD FOLD-IN

Many wonder how there can be a just and caring God, when this horrible, nauseating ordeal persists. The screams are deafening and the stories are unbelievable – it's nearly impossible to avoid, yet only a fraction of Americans are disgusted by it. And the White House seems to endorse it! To find out where madness and violent outbursts are the order of the day, fold page in as shown.

FOLD PAGE OVER LIKE THIS!

A ▸ FOLD PAGE OVER LEFT ◂ B FOLD BACK SO THAT "A" MEETS "B"

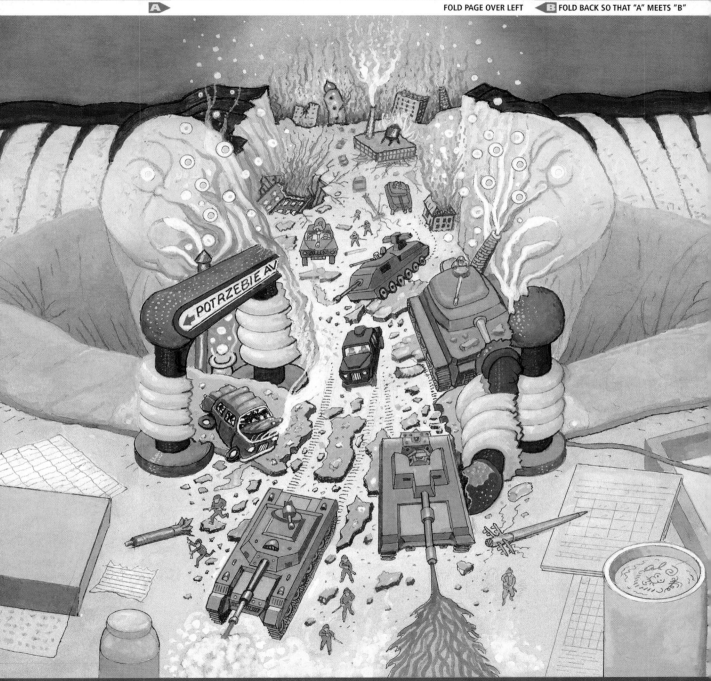

ALL WAR IS DISASTROUS. POLITICIANS GIVE COMPLEX JUSTIFICATIONS FOR IT. BOMBERS, TANKS AND DRONES INFLICT GREAT DAMAGE TO ENTIRE POPULATIONS. SO WE MUST END WARMONGERS' CONTROL OF OUR FEARS

A ◂ WRITER AND ARTIST: AL JAFFEE ▸ B

THE WITCH HUNT

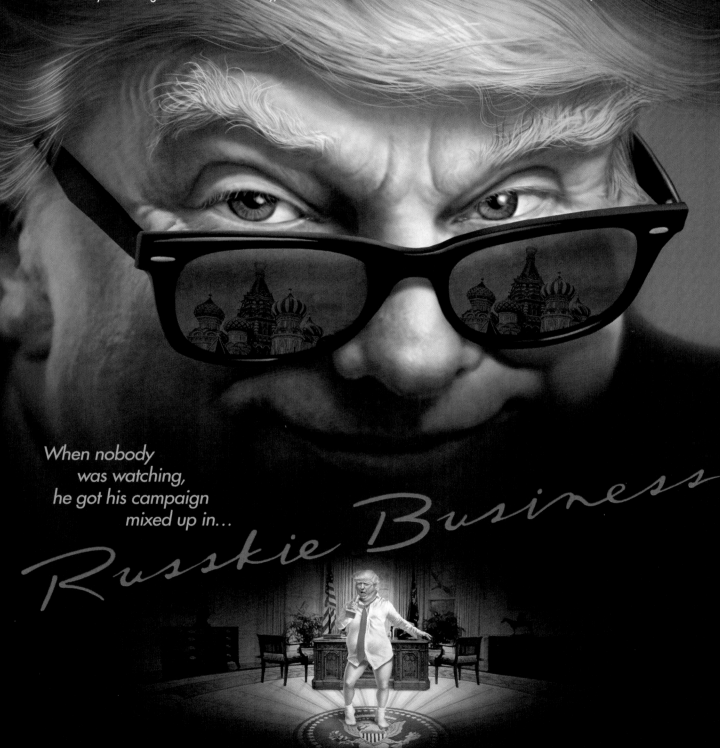

TEAM TRUMP COLLUDES WITH RUSSIANS
THE AGE OF TREASON

To quote President Trump, "нет российского сговора"—"There is no Russian collusion!" And we believe him! Okay, there *were* numerous secret meetings between Russians and Trump officials that were first denied, but then later owned up to. And *maybe* Jared Kushner forgot to list the names on his security clearance form of a few hundred foreigners he met with. Mistakes happen! And who cares if Trump fired the FBI Director to get him off the Russian investigation? And who's George Papadopoulos, anyway? The important point is that no "smoking gun" has yet been uncovered (unless you count that whole email exchange between Donald Jr. and some shadowy Russian figure with "dirt" on Hillary). THERE WAS NO COLLUSION—PERIOD! Now, comrades, who's up for some borscht?

When nobody
was watching,
he got his campaign
mixed up in…

Russkie Business

THE REPUBLICAN PARTY Presents A TRUMP CAMPAIGN Production "RUSSKIE BUSINESS"
DONALD TRUMP   DONALD TRUMP JR.   MICHAEL FLYNN   GEORGE PAPADOPOULOS   CARTER PAGE
JEFF SESSIONS   SERGEY KISLYAK   with ROBERT MUELLER as THE NEMESIS
(Most Likely) Directed by DONALD TRUMP

R | RUSSIAN MEDDLING

ARTIST: MARK FREDRICKSON

"And he's not like those other dictators.
He writes me beautiful letters."

WRITER & ARTIST **IVAN EHLERS**

WRITER **KIT LIVELY**   ARTIST **LUKE MCGARRY**

"You can come out, sir. It's not really the bad man."

WRITER & ARTIST **IVAN EHLERS**

"One last thing...Barron is running for Class President next month..."

I'm Mr. Trump's attorney and this is my attorney.
Once his attorney arrives, we can begin.

WRITER & ARTIST **JASON CHATFIELD**

WHY JARED KUSHNER SECRETLY MET WITH THE RUSSIAN AMBASSADOR

He and Ivanka just couldn't get their borscht to come out right

Trump asked him to squeeze it in between negotiating a Palestinian agreement, hashing out a North Korea strategy and signing him up for Hulu

He was inquiring about job openings in the Russian government, because his current gig just isn't working out

He wanted to give the Russians a heads-up that his father-in-law is bats#!t crazy

The whole thing was actually a coincidental Grindr hookup

ARTIST **ANTON EMDIN**

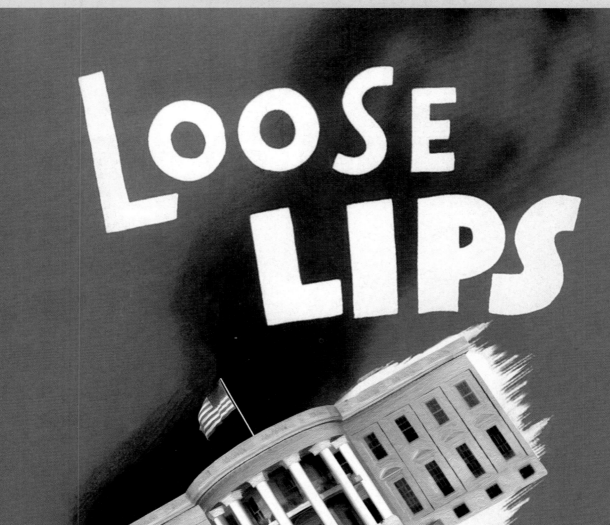

WHAT'S ON VLADIMIR PUTIN'S DESK?

Blu-Ray of *Rocky IV* edited so that Ivan Drago wins

Continuous live feed with close associate

Vlad's To-Do List:
~~Annex Crimea~~
Poison enemies
Practice menacing smirk in mirror
Send birthday card to Assad
Invade Latvia
DVR *This Is Us*
Pick up dry cleaning

OLIGARCH ASSN.
CERTIFICATE OF APPRECIATION
V. PUTIN

PAUL MANAFORT WOULD LIKE TO CONNECT VIA LinkedIn

Gift from when Mike Flynn visited

Blood-stained letter opener

Paperweight made from Patriots owner Robert Kraft's stolen Super Bowl ring

That button you press to make the guy sitting in front of you fall into a pool of piranhas

May Day gift from his secretary

WRITER: MIKE MORSE
ARTIST: WARD SUTTON

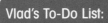

THREE MONTHS LATER

WRITER & ARTIST **LARS KENSETH**

A series of memos written earlier this year by former FBI Director James Comey described serious and questionable statements and actions made by President Trump during their meetings. What they didn't include, however, were these even more explosive revelations, which MAD is leaking here for the first time as...

STATEMENTS FROM THE

As I entered, he was wrapping up a **photo op** with some **Boy Scouts**, with whom he had just shared **all** of the **nuclear launch codes**.

He **then** asked if I could somehow make it that **all female bureau agents** wear selections from the **Ivanka fashion line** exclusively...

His deal was **simple:** drop the case against **Mike Flynn** and the job hosting *Celebrity Apprentice* was **mine**.

...also in this meeting were **Jared Kushner**, a **dwarf** in a **kilt** and **Baba Booey** from the **Howard Stern program**.

Then, appearing to be speaking to **no one** in **particular**, the President **wistfully wondered** if it was possible to **fabricate DNA evidence** to show that **Eric** wasn't really **his** son...

I thought it was an **odd question**: "What kind of **money** are we talking about to **take out Jake Tapper?**"

When I mentioned it seemed that the **smell** of **boiling cabbage** had **permeated** the Oval Office, Mr. Trump's one-word response was "**Bannon**."

Making reference to my **6'8" height**, President Trump insisted it was **he** who originated the phrase "**a tall drink of water.**" He then **also** took credit for inventing the phrases "**Prime the pump**," "Thank God it's Friday," and "**YOLO**."

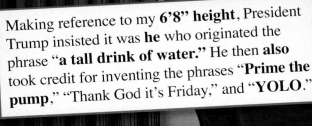

REDACTED

COMEY MEMOS

ARTIST:
TOM RICHMOND

His **thinly-veiled** threat was **chilling**: "I could stand in the **middle** of the Oval Office and **shoot** the Director of the FBI in the **head** and I wouldn't **lose voters**."

He seemed **surprised** when I confessed to not knowing the **overnight ratings** for *Dancing with the Stars*.

...at which point he took out a **solid gold yo-yo** and floundered through a **pathetic** "walk the dog." He then proclaimed himself "the **greatest** yo-yo guy **ever**" and urged me to "just ask **anyone**."

He spoke at length about "**outdated**" and "**lame**" laws preventing Americans from **marrying** their **daughters**.

20 minutes into **my briefing** he asked me, "**Which** one are **you** again?"

Despite the President's **assurances** that dessert consisted of "the **most beautiful** piece of chocolate cake that you've **ever** seen," I found it to be "**meh**."

At one point, the President said, "Even my **farts** smell **great**" — and then he **farted** to prove it. I didn't have the **courage** to tell him how **wrong** he was.

The **loyalty oath** Mr. Trump demanded I take sounded as if it was **directly plagiarized** from the **opening theme** to the *Friends* TV show.

Suddenly he **blurted out**, "Who knew sharing **highly classified intel** with the Russians would be **so complicated?**"

THINGS TRUMP AND PUTIN
AGREED/DISAGREED ABOUT
AT THEIR G20 MEETING

Whether *Morning Joe* co-host Mika Brzezinski is hot or not.....DISAGREED

If Trump uses more WWE footage to make memes, he cannot
show any in which he dominates Nikolai Volkoff.....AGREED

Which Property Brother is cuter.....DISAGREED

Russian prostitutes are among the best in the world!....AGREED

Whether physical or emotional intimidation
is a more effective negotiating tactic.....DISAGREED

At the end of every FOX News interview, Trump must tug his
left earlobe as a secret signal of affection for Putin.....AGREED

That it will be harder in 2020 to hack and swing
the election in Trump's favor, but still doable.....AGREED

ARTIST **ANTON EMDIN**

FROM THE GUYS WHO BROUGHT YOU THE WORST PRESIDENCY EVER

DONALD
TRUMP

DONALD
TRUMP JR.

JARED
KUSHNER

there's something about russia

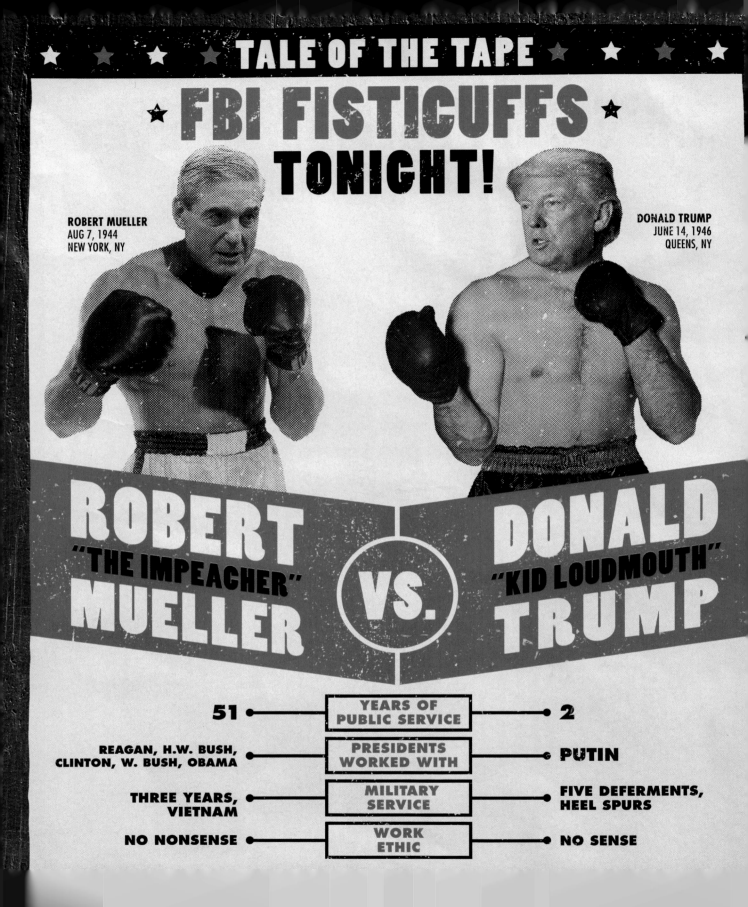

"Our intelligence agencies say Finnish Well Goblin eats children that get too close to the old well. But I will tell you he was very strong and powerful in his denial today. So, really, we're all to blame."

WRITER & ARTIST **LARS KENSETH**

CONCLUSIVE PROOF RUSSIA HACKED THE DNC

Every leaked John Podesta email included a different borscht recipe

Strong evidence suggests Hillary Clinton's private server contained a bootleg cut of *Rocky IV* in which Drago wins

Every night, the White House has GrubHub-ordered goulash deliveries showing up that no one placed

DNC Chair Debbie Wasserman Schultz hates Anton Chekov, yet every time she logs onto Amazon, three of his books are in her shopping cart

Last time anyone checked, all the nuclear code passwords had been changed to "YakovSmirnoff5"

ARTIST **WARD SUTTON**

THE REAL REASONS RUSSIA WAS BANNED FROM THE WINTER OLYMPICS

Trump would've had a real dilemma deciding which country to root for

The IOC figured that if Putin wanted a medal badly enough, he could always just take one from a weaker country

A hot mic caught Putin saying what everyone else was thinking: Nobody gives a s#!t about the Winter Olympics

It was felt that Russia would be better served by focusing its vast cheating energies on wrecking America's democracy

It's to give the appearance that someone is being tough on Russia

Putin's ice-dancing outfits were just getting too damn sexy

TRUMP PANDERS TO PUTIN AT HELSINKI MEETING

THE SUMMIT OF ALL FEARS

When Donald Trump and Vladimir Putin met behind closed doors in Helsinki, it seemed a little fishy. When Trump later stood with Putin at a press conference and said, "I don't see any reason why it would be" Russia who meddled in the 2016 election, it seemed even fishier! Trump's toadying response to Putin's claims of innocence was condemned by lawmakers, and the president was forced to walk back his comments, claiming he meant to say he didn't "see any reason why it wouldn't be Russia." We celebrate one of our country's finest unpresidential moments with this timeless keepsake...

The Badford Exchange Presents

The Helsinki Summit 2018

COMMEMORATIVE PLATE

Commemorate the landmark dog and pony show between America's leader, Vladimir Putin, and his lapdog, Donald Trump, with this extremely strong and powerful hand-numbered treasure!

A collage of skillfully rendered images depicts the easy Top-Bottom rapport between two super-narcissists on the day our Commander In Chief flushed his intelligence community down the туалет!

SEAL OF THE BADFORD EXCHANGE FAUXTHENTICITY

This limited edition fine porcelain plate features:

- **An intricate border of inlaid hammer and sickle symbols.**

- **An easel with one leg shorter than the other to display your plate on unequal footing for the entire world to see!**

- **A limited edition of only 1,500 plates. (But some are saying 150,000, making it the biggest commemorative plate in American history. Much bigger than Obama's plate.)**

Make Your Curio Cabinet Great Again by Ordering Today!

WRITER **TERESA BURNS PARKHURST**   ARTIST **PAUL SHIPPER**

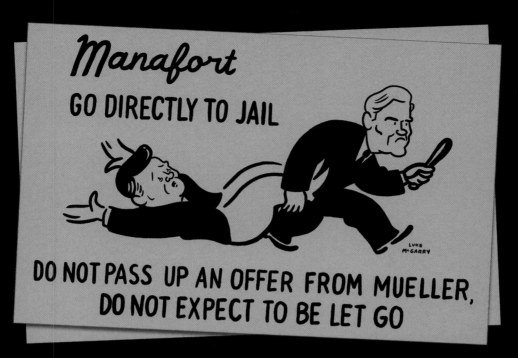

FLYNN'S TURNED

(Sung to the tune of "The Flintstones")

Flynn's turned! Michael Flynn's turned,
Mueller nailed him for his per-ju-ry
Flipped him, like a pancake
For his role in the con-spi-ra-cy!

Last year, he was chanting "Lock her up!"
Next year, he'll expose the cover-up!

Now that Michael Flynn's turned,
Looks like Jared's gonna do time
Collusion's a crime
Trump could be screwed this time!

PLEA DEAL

donald
trump

robert
mueller

Matthew Whitaker
Directed by ~~Jeff Sessions~~

catch me
if you can

The True Story
behind the
Fake News

WRITER & ARTIST **IVAN EHLERS**

It has become a tradition in our country for an outgoing President to leave behind a letter for the incoming President that offers congratulations, support and wisdom. Given the White House's current resident, we're curious about the kind of letter the NEXT President will receive (in three years, or hopefully, less!) So please pardon us (see what we did there?) as we wistfully contemplate…

Donald Trump's L

FAKE

THE TWEET STOPS HERE.

Make America Grab Again!

Crooked Hillary Has Fat Ankles.

WRITER: STAN SINBERG   ARTIST: BOB STAAKE

THE WHITE HOUSE
WASHINGTON

Dear Incoming President,

Congratulations on your victory. While it wasn't as historic as mine, which was the biggest electoral win since Reagan, you still won. And don't feel bad that your inauguration crowd didn't match mine, which was the biggest ever, despite those fake news photos "proving" otherwise.

Welcome to the White House, even though it's a dump. I mean it was a dump when I got here, that's what a lot of people were saying. So, I gold-plated everything and now it's the most beautiful it's ever been, going all the way back to George Washington.

I'm a very intelligent person, okay? Very intelligent. So, I would say it's probably a good idea, a very good idea, if you take my advice.

Hire only the best people, the kind who will give you a loyalty pledge and not recuse themselves if you're under investigation, or flip on you if they're threatened with jail time. I strongly recommend family members.

Remember, and many many people have said this: collusion is not a crime — not that there was any collusion, and I think I would know.

No matter how great you make America, you are only a temporary custodian of this office, so monetize your brand. By the way, have you tried my bottled water or men's fragrance?

Continue to drain the swamp by not filling vacant posts in government agencies. When the agencies fail, cite that as proof of their incompetence. It's a big win-win.

Whatever you do, don't release your taxes.

Putin: Great guy. The best.

A big part of your job will be working with Congress, and I have to say it, because it's politically incorrect: you can't trust a senator with brain cancer. I like senators who don't have brain cancer, all right?

Make threats, blame others and take lots of credit. It works. When accused of something terrible, deny it and change the subject, especially if you did it. Never apologize.

The best time to tweet is between five and six in the morning while on the toilet. The second-best time is a bit later, to repeat something you heard while watching "Fox And Friends." As long as you have that show, you don't need a cabinet.

As incoming President, you are free to set your own course, but why would you want to when you can follow MY brilliant course? I accomplished a lot, actually more than anyone, which was unbelievable. Just unbelievable.

Covfefe,

[signature]

P.S. Take some time to play a little golf now and then. I am attaching a list of my golf courses, which are the best and most beautiful in the world.

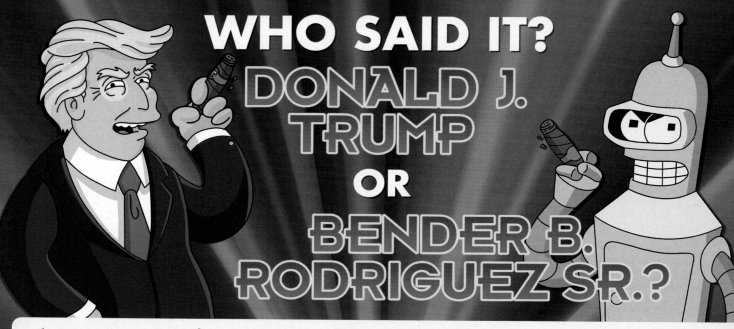

WHO SAID IT?
DONALD J. TRUMP
OR
BENDER B. RODRIGUEZ SR.?

1. "Game's over, losers! I have all the money!"

2. "The whole world must learn of our peaceful ways, by force!"

3. "I bet I can eat nachos and go to the bathroom at the same time!"

4. "This is the worst kind of discrimination there is: the kind against me!"

5. "Anything less than immortality is a complete waste of time."

6. "You're a pimple on society's ass and you'll never amount to anything!"

7. "You know what cheers me up? Other people's misfortune."

8. "How can I be so bad at everything I try, and still be so great?"

9. "He struck a chord with the voters when he pledged not to go on a killing spree."

10. "Some of us have real problems! I just learned there are people with fancier sausage meats than me!"

11. "Survived the heart attack?! Damn you Obamacare!"

BENDER: 1, 2, 3, 4, 5, 6, 7, 8, 9, 10, 11
(but admit it, you thought some of them were from Trump!)

The Fast Five
WAYS TO CONVINCE TRUMP CLIMATE CHANGE IS REAL

1. Explain that, while it may not affect him in his lifetime, it will affect Barron, and Barron's children — and then explain who Barron is

2. Put the central air in Trump Tower on "low," but tell him it's on "high"

3. Tell him that it'll cause widespread extinctions long before Donald Jr. gets a chance to kill everything himself

4. Have climate-change believers donate more money to his re-election campaign than climate-change deniers

5. Warn him that higher, drier temperatures would make his hair a target for wildfires

Artist: Alejandro Rivas

OVERHEARD AT TRUMP'S MEETING WITH POPE FRANCIS

Writers: Charlie Kadau and Jacob Lambert
Artist: Bob Staake

Not every public figure flaunts their body art like Angelina Jolie—and for good reasons (one being not every *body* is like Angelina Jolie's). Some celebs consider their tats too troubling to ever unveil. Well, consider us troublemakers, because we're about to bare these...

EMBARRASSING CELEBRITY TATTOOS

VLADIMIR PUTIN
INKED: THE MOMENT HE FELT THE URGE TO KICK AMERICA'S ASS (AGE 8).

GISELE (A.K.A. MRS. TOM BRADY)
INKED: AFTER THE LAST SUPER BOWL.

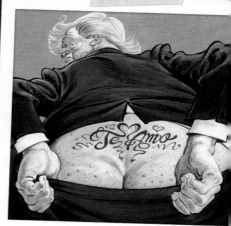

DONALD TRUMP
INKED: REFUSES TO DIVULGE (BUT IT'S PARTLY WHY HE'S BUILDING A WALL ON THE MEXICAN BORDER).

JEFF BEZOS
INKED: IN 1994, TO REMEMBER HIS FIRST AMAZON PASSWORD.

MIKE PENCE
INKED: DURING THE ONE REBELLIOUS WEEK OF HIS TEENS.

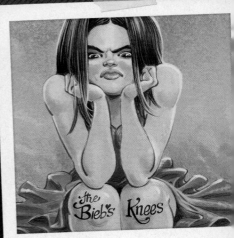

SELENA GOMEZ
INKED: ONE OF THE TIMES SHE CRAWLED BACK TO JUSTIN BIEBER

WRITER: **JEFF KRUSE**   ARTIST: **GIDEON KENDALL**

PRESIDENT'S SUMMER READING LIST

These are all untouched, unread, and collecting dust as Donald J. Trump does not and will not read, *but* if he *did,* it would be the most tremendous reading you've ever seen (his words).

WRITERS **ALEXIS NOVAK & JASON CHATFIELD**   **ARTIST** **JASON CHATFIELD**

From 1966 through 1992, Paul Coker illustrated a feature we call "Horrifying Clichés." It's the ghoulish game in which Paul interpreted phrases or expressions to create never-before-seen monsters. After 15 installments, it seemed his fiendish work was done. But now there's a new gruesome, lumpy monster roaming the land, and it's become necessary to play the first — and hopefully the last — round of...

HORRIFYING CLICHÉS

SPECIAL TRUMP EDITION

WRITER: DESMOND DEVLIN   **ARTIST: PAUL COKER**

Releasing **HATEFUL TWEETS**

Making A **FALSE CLAIM**

Exposing **HIS IGNORANCE**

Dividing **A NATION**

The Boy Scout Law
Rewritten by Donald Trump

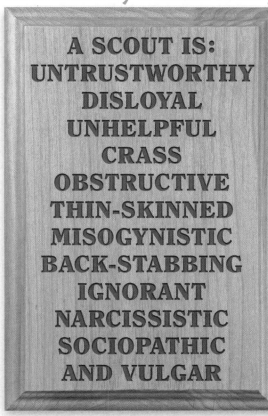

A SCOUT IS:
UNTRUSTWORTHY
DISLOYAL
UNHELPFUL
CRASS
OBSTRUCTIVE
THIN-SKINNED
MISOGYNISTIC
BACK-STABBING
IGNORANT
NARCISSISTIC
SOCIOPATHIC
AND VULGAR

Trump's I.Q. Test

100,000 people are in Crowd A. 50,000 people are in Crowd B. How much smaller is Crowd B?
A) 25%
B) 50%
C) Crowd B is huge, the biggest in the history of crowds

When out with a lady, it is considered proper to grab her...
A) A drink
B) A chair
C) P***y

Define "adversary" in the following sentence:
"Russia is an adversary of America."
A) Mortal enemy
B) Dishonest foe
C) Trustworthy ally

Boyfriend : Girlfriend ::
A) Uncle : Aunt
B) Husband : Wife
C) Father : Daughter

Complete this sentence: "Despite the constant negative press...
A) I will continue to work my hardest."
B) I refuse to be deterred from what I believe is right."
C) Covfefe."

Puerto Rico is:
A) 1,000 miles from the U.S. Mainland
B) 2.5 hours from Miami, by air
C) In the middle of the ocean, virtually impossible to reach

MAD PRESENTS...*UNLESS*

Experts agree that running can add years to your life...

UNLESS

you're an African-American who was just pulled over by white cops.

Watching YouTube videos while working is a harmless way to alleviate stress...

UNLESS

you're an Uber driver.

Society's change in attitude is making life better for the LGBTQ community...

UNLESS

you're a trans person who has to pee in North Carolina.

Spontaneously writing whatever comes into your head is an excellent method for purging anger without negative consequences...

UNLESS

you're the President of the United States.

Writer: Mike Morse   Artist: John Kerschbaum

"And we're sure none of them are criminals or unknown Middle Easterners?"

WRITER & ARTIST **IVAN EHLERS**

THINGS BEING SAID BY THE HALL OF PRESIDENTS'
ANIMATRONIC TRUMP

TRUMP'S MUSLIM TRAVEL BAN
MAKE AMERICA HATE AGAIN

While running for President, candidate Trump promised he would ban Muslims from entering the U.S.—an idea so un-American, even a C-level, middle-school civics student would know it was unconstitutional. Once President, Trump tried again and again to ban Muslims from countries he didn't like—and each time, the ban was swatted down by the courts. His latest ruse was to add non-Muslim North Korea to the list, a country whose people are dying from starvation, not an urge to visit Epcot. Throughout this travesty, the Trump administration has insisted it's not "a ban" (much in the same way that "enhanced interrogation" isn't torture). But they're not fooling anyone—especially those in affected nations when they try to book travel to Trump's America.

The no-travel site for people living in countries who have been capriciously and arbitrarily banned from entering the United States!

trumpelocity

CHAD! IRAN! NORTH KOREA! LIBYA! SOMALIA! SYRIA! YEMEN!

At Trumpelocity, you save big – really big – on travel to America! That's because I'm not letting you in!

The bright lights of New York City! YOU'RE NOT GONNA SEE 'EM!

The historic U.S. Capitol— you think I'm gonna let you near where I live? FUGGEDABOUDIT!

The awe-inspiring majesty of the Grand Canyon— look at it in a book, because YOU'RE NOT COMING!

How many traveling?
I'll tell you how many – ZERO!

Dates of travel?
How about the First of May-be-You-Should-Stay-Home to the Tenth of Nope-vember??

Rental car needed?
Of course not!

SAUDI ARABIA! DUBAI! QATAR! TURKEY! UNITED ARAB EMIRATES!

Go to www.you'reinvited.com if you live in one of the Muslim-majority nations listed above. You'll be redirected to a REAL travel site because even though terrorists have originated in your country, you can visit the U.S. any time you want! The fact that your nation just happens to have Trump-branded properties in them is PURELY coincidental!

WRITER: CHARLIE KADAU
SCULPTOR: LIZ LOMAX

TRUMPELOCITY — WE MAKE NOT TRAVELING UNCONSTITUTIONAL!™

TRUMPTY DUMPTY
A NURSERY RHYME UPDATE

*Trumpty Dumpty
cries for a wall,*

*Trumpty says
he'll shut down it all,*

*America's women
and America's men*

*Wonder if Trumpty
is lying again.*

ARTIST **SAM SISCO**

Remember when greeting cards were great? Back in their heyday, if you wanted to let someone know you remembered their birthday or were sad because they lost a loved one, greeting cards got the job done. And they did it with style and flair! Today's liberals have let our precious greeting card industry fall into ruin. But fear not! Our president is going to...

MAKE AMERICA GREET AGAIN

new american greetings
by donald trump

WRITER AND ARTIST **TERESA BURNS PARKHURST**

GET WELL

Message Inside:
Many illnesses are preventable. I, myself, have never been sick. Never. I am probably the healthiest person there is, without a doubt.

Message Inside:
Believe me, you are not aging well.
You should consider getting some work done.

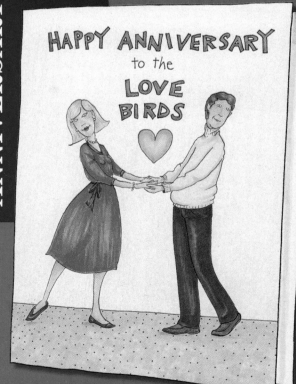

Message Inside:
No one has more respect for the institution of marriage than me, and I mean NO one.
I have had several very beautiful wives.
Gorgeous, in fact.

89

NEW BABY

CONGRATULATIONS ON YOUR NEW LITTLE BUNDLE OF JOY!

Message Inside:
Babies are just great, aren't they? But, I am telling you because I KNOW, they completely ruin a woman's vagina. True.

MOTHER'S DAY

HAPPY MOTHER'S DAY

Message Inside:
Being a mother has got to be a truly magnificent feeling! Very happy for you! (Too bad about your vagina.)

RETIREMENT

ENJOY YOUR RETIREMENT

Message Inside:
Retiring is a good deal for people who are lazy. An incredibly good deal for the lazy-do-nothings! I like people who DON'T retire.

GRADUATION

CONGRATULATIONS ON EARNING YOUR DEGREE!

Message Inside:
The crowd at my graduation ceremony? The biggest in history! It's true, ask anyone. They went absolutely nuts when I crossed the stage. Totally nuts for me.

VALENTINE'S DAY

VALENTINE

Be mine

Message Inside:
I have a tremendous number of valentines, and they let me do anything I want to them. I can just grab them like a bowling ball...wait, that's three holes—are there three holes? Anyway, I have zero, ZERO problems getting a valentine.

HANUKKAH

HAPPY HANUKKAH

Message Inside:
The Jews love me. And they're so funny, really funny people. Hilarious, even. I've discovered that many comedians are Jews. Really, they are. They spell things strangely, but good, funny people.

SO VERY SORRY FOR YOUR LOSS

Message Inside:
Your loved one being dead makes it very uncomfortable for other people. They just don't know what to say. Trying to make you feel better is very difficult. Impossible, actually. Not good.

...and unto the world the CHRIST CHILD was BORN!

Message Inside:
Listen to me when I tell you that many, many people say how much I remind them of Jesus! Not the baby one, and not the one on the cross— he was so dirty from all the, well, there were thorns and blood and sweating. I'm like the good-looking one with the fabulous hair.

POSTCARD FROM A STATE OF DESPERATION

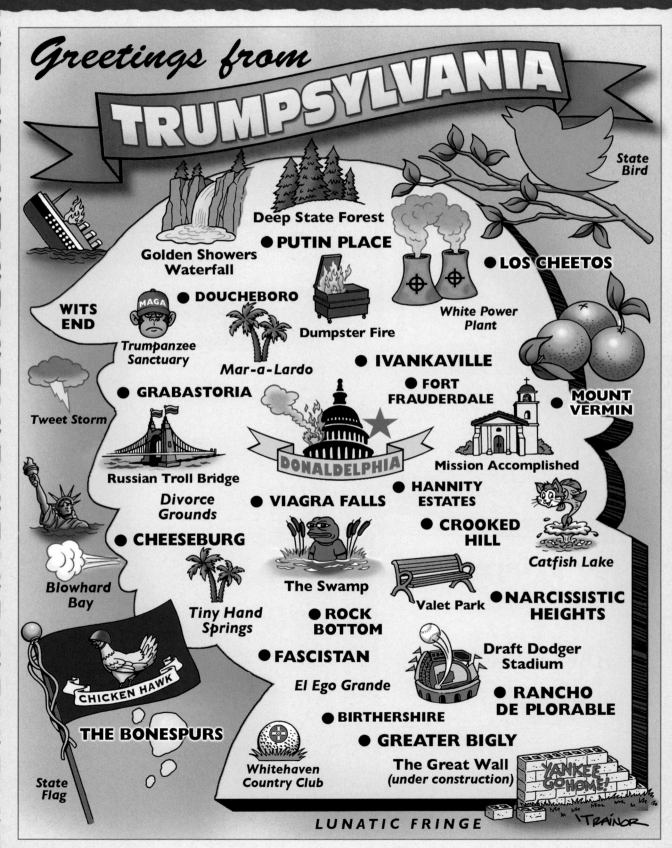

Greetings from

TRUMPSYLVANIA

State Bird

Deep State Forest

● PUTIN PLACE

Golden Showers Waterfall

● LOS CHEETOS

WITS END

● DOUCHEBORO

White Power Plant

Trumpanzee Sanctuary

Mar-a-Lardo

Dumpster Fire

● IVANKAVILLE

● FORT FRAUDERDALE

MOUNT VERMIN

● GRABASTORIA

Tweet Storm

DONALDELPHIA

Russian Troll Bridge

Mission Accomplished

Divorce Grounds

● VIAGRA FALLS

● HANNITY ESTATES

● CROOKED HILL

Catfish Lake

● CHEESEBURG

The Swamp

Valet Park

●NARCISSISTIC HEIGHTS

Blowhard Bay

Tiny Hand Springs

● ROCK BOTTOM

Draft Dodger Stadium

● FASCISTAN

El Ego Grande

● RANCHO DE PLORABLE

CHICKEN HAWK

● BIRTHERSHIRE

THE BONESPURS

● GREATER BIGLY

Whitehaven Country Club

The Great Wall (under construction)

YANKEE GO HOME!

State Flag

LUNATIC FRINGE

TRAINOR

SUGGESTED PHRASES FOR THE NEW TALKING DONALD TRUMP DOLL

Robin, see if you can get me a 2:30 appointment at Supercuts.

All this Mexican — ooh, Trump's gotsta take a dump!

I got your Trump Tower right here!

'Mrs. Omarosa Trump'! I like the sound of that!

Me, an egomaniac?!? Dr. Chompsky, you're fired!

George, Carolyn, I'll give you a million dollars to do a horizontal merger on the boardroom table!

I'm sorry my check bounced, Marla.

Oh, crap! I'm bankrupt again?!?

I'm sorry my check bounced, Ivana.

Melania, what do you mean you want to name our child Kwame?

Ooh — a penny!

All right, I admit it, I slept with Leona Helmsley — and it was the best sex I ever had!

WE DON'T KNOW IF THIS IS GOOD OR BAD FOR US...

SUBSCRIBE TO MAD

GAMBLING ODDS ON FUTURE TEXTS
FROM DONALD TRUMP

WRITER **JON GUTIERREZ**

FEMA is about to unveil a new "Presidential Alert" system that will allow Trump to text all our phones with emergency information. It'll be like an Amber Alert, only somehow...more alarming. Here are our odds on just what "Trump emergency texts" you'll be wishing you could opt out of in the near future!

5:1

NO TOILET PAPER IN "PRESIDENTIAL TWEET ROOM!"

25:1

HELP! Thirsty, but "Diet Coke Button" is all GUNKED UP! Someone call ARMY CORPS OF ENGINEERS and tell them to get over here with a SIX PACK, PRONTO!

30:1

CAN'T SHUT OFF SELF-TANNER SPRAY! Went from "COOL RANCH" to "BLAZE!" SEND HELP before I get to "JACKED: HOT WINGS!"

35:1

TV STOPPED WORKING! With no Fox & Friends, how will I know how awesome I'm doing? Or learn about "friends?"

50:1

CALL THE POLICE! Went to meet some "ambassador" but there's a FOREIGN GUY IN THERE!

THE STARTLING SIMILARITIES AND DIFFERENCES BETWEEN

PRESIDENT TRUMP AND CAPTAIN UNDERPANTS

ARTIST **SARAH CHALEK**

	TRUMP	CAPTAIN
• Clearly has nothing to hide....................	○	✓
• His incompetence is part of his charm....................	○	✓
• Seems to have a split personality....................	✓	✓
• Is currently being blackmailed by Russia....................	✓	○
• Is a bizarre cartoon character who looks like he was created by manic eight-year-olds....................	✓	✓
• Could save the world....................	○	✓

WRITER & ARTIST **NOAH VAN SCIVER**

"Whoa, slow down, egghead!"

WRITER & ARTIST **IVAN EHLERS**

EXPLORATION.
PROTECTION.
DISTRACTION.

United States of America
SPACE FORCE
APPLICATION FOR EMPLOYMENT

Thank you for your interest in joining the Trump Space Force.
While we're still in the process of ~~figuring out what the hell we're doing~~ developing
the Trump Space Force, we appreciate your interest in this great distraction endeavor!

SPACE FORCE
EXPLORATION.
PROTECTION.
DISTRACTION.

PERSONALITY TEST

How much of a distraction could you make in a news cycle?
- Slightly distracting
- Very distracting
- Shoot someone on Fifth Avenue" distracting

Please name five things the Trump Space Force could be worth the time/effort/money spent on it:
_____
_____
_____
_____
_____

Ok, one thing.... ? Anything at all?
Like, you'd buy a hat with the logo on it, right? _____

How do you feel about Aliens? _____
How about those other Aliens? _____
You know the ones we mean, right? (WINK!)   Y / N

**Which of these space threats would
you be willing to fight:**
- Aliens
- Martians
- Justin Trudeau's Heavenly Smile

How did you hear about the Trump Space Force?
- Read about it in an official Presidential "crapper tweet"
- "Cellmate gossip" from Paul Manafort
- From a misspelled protest sign, like all my news
- Heard 4-year-old say what a dumb idea it was
- In between screams of "Lock Her Up!"
- Anchors on Fox & Friends screamed about it while orgasm-ing

PHYSICAL QUALIFICATIONS

o you own your own spacecraft?   Y / N

so, can we use it?   Y / N (Note: You will not be reimbursed.)

ave you ever fired a laser gun?   Y / N

you did, wouldn't it be cool?   Y / HELL Y

en you make laser gun sounds with your mouth, what sound do you use?
"Pew! Pew"
"Zap! Zap!"
"Laser gun! Laser gun!" (like the President does!)

Name _____
Signature _____
Date _____

"In Space, No One Can Hear You Scream About The Mueller Investigation"

PLANNED PROVISIONS OF TRUMPCARE

Health insurers will not be allowed to deny coverage to anyone, except Muslims, Mexicans, members of the media, and Hillary Clint

Trump will personally administer all breast examinations

Doctors will be required to refer to patients dying from terminal diseases as "losers"

Narcissistic-sociopathic disorder will no longer be recognized as an incapacitating mental illness

There will be higher Medicare reimbursements for doctors who have Fox News on their waiting room TVs

WRITER **EVAN WAITE**   ARTIST **BOB STAAKE**

HOW TO SPOT FAKE NEWS

Overly-sensationalist headline contains five or more emojis

The URL FakeNewz.biz seems suspicious. Wouldn't a legitimate media outlet have sprung for FakeNewz.*com*?

The article is written in a Choose-Your-Own-Adventure format, allowing you to select the outcome that best fits your personal political agenda

It was shared with you on Facebook by that weird old guy whose friend request you only accepted because you thought he was your distant uncle, and now you're afraid to unfriend him because he's holding an AR-15 in all his profile pics

The article repeatedly misspells "Lizard People"

When you add up all the slices on the pie chart, the total comes out to 317.9%

For a news outlet with millions of Twitter follower it sure seems odd that whe you call the number listed The Poughkeepsie Truth-Telle page, you get a Pizza Hut

Not only do none of the quotations cite a source, they're all lifted word-for-word from Billy Joel's "We Didn't Start the Fire"

The story is being yelled at you by a pale, sweaty White House press secretary wearing a much larger man's suit jacket

Writer: Kenny Keil   Artist: Ward Sutton

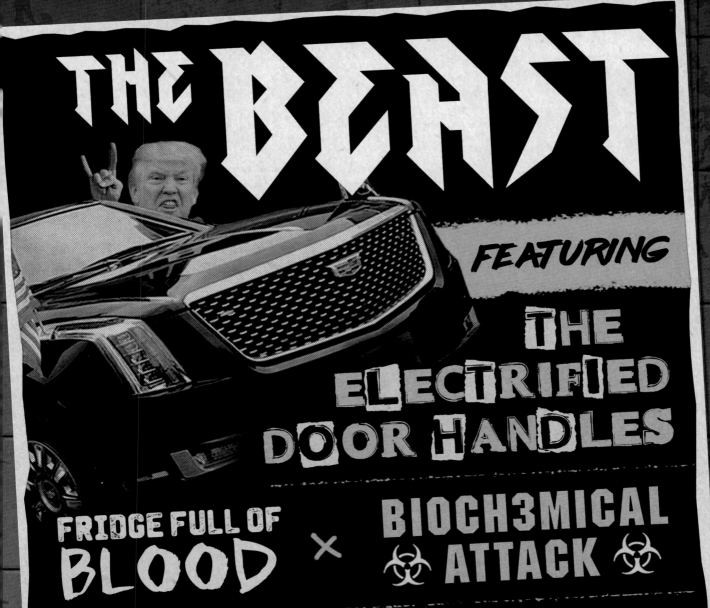

THE **BEAST**

FEATURING

THE ELECTRIFIED DOOR HANDLES

FRIDGE FULL OF **BLOOD** × **BIOCH3MICAL ATTACK**

SMOKE SCREENZ × SEALED AGAINST × BACK-UP **LIMO!**

BREAKING NEWS
PAHOA VOLCANO ERUPTION

LIVE
CNN
4:20 PM EST

ORANGE MAGMA FLOWS THROUGH STREETS OF HAWAII

"Another day of the raging orange menace that destroys everything in its path.

Also, a volcano has erupted in Hawaii."

WRITER & ARTIST **JASON CHATFIELD**   SPECIAL THANKS **SCOTT DOOLEY**

A BREAKDOWN OF TRUMP'S 30 MILLION TWITTER FOLLOWERS

Trump himself, under many, many, different screen names
11%

Cabinet members terrified of what will happen if they *don't* follow him
4%

Die-hard supporters, awaiting Dear Leader's revealing of Truth
27%

Grammar geeks eagerly waiting for more mangled syntax they can triumphantly point out
9%

College students doing research for Abnormal Psychology class
6%

White nationalists
12%
(Yeah, we thought it was closer to 50%, too)

Shadowy characters with Twitter handles like "Ivanov2016" and "BorschtBabe"
13%

Investigators working for Robert Mueller, astonished at how easy their job is becoming
4%

Contestants in an impeachment betting pool
14%

Fake news reporters, out to distort whatever the President says in order to make him look bad, because they hate America
0%

WRITER **JEFF KRUSE**   ARTIST **BOB STAAKE**

EVEN MORE THING TRUMP RUINED

 RED CAPS

 DIET COKE

 IVANKA'S BRAN

 ANYTHING ORANGE

 TWITTER

 CHOCOLATE CAI

 TIKI TORCHES

 HOME ALONE 2

 NATIONAL PARI

WRITER & ARTIST **MARIA SCRIVAN**

TRUMP ON TWITTER ANTISOCIAL MEDIA

When Twitter started in 2006, its creators admitted that they weren't exactly sure how it would be used. Sadly, now we know. It turns out that Twitter is the perfect weapon of mass distraction for President Trump to spill his misinformed, inflammatory, misguided, false and flat-out dangerous rantings. Apparently, Trump's favorite time to tweet is during one of his Presidential dumps. Ahh—take a deep breath: you can almost smell the stench as you read each 140-character expulsion of verbal diarrhea. How does our Tweeter-in-Chief do it day after day? Perhaps the answer can be found in his choice of breakfast food.

GET THE ENERGY YOU NEED TO SEND WILD, IRRESPONSIBLE TWEETS AT THREE A.M.!

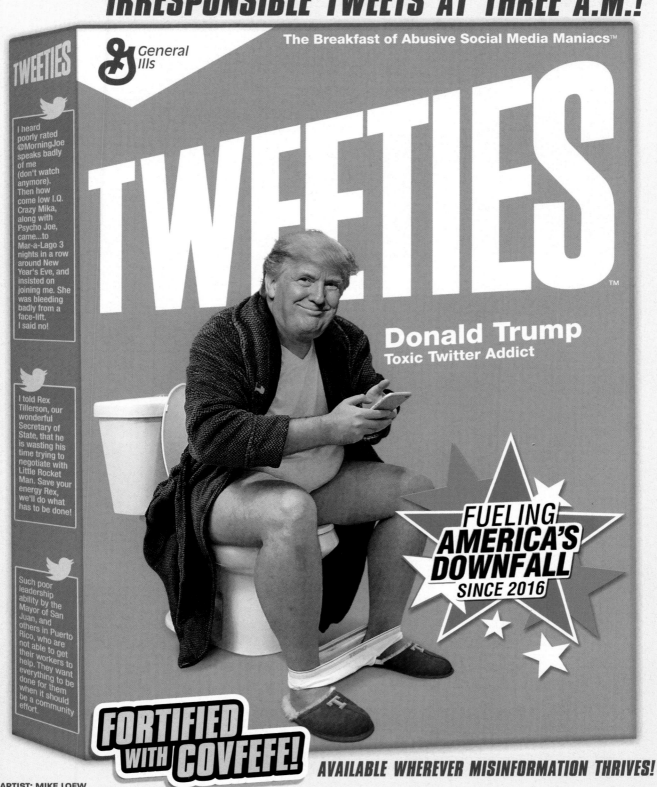

TRUMP ARTIST: MIKE LOEW

101

TRUMP'S SPACE FORCE ONE MISSTEP FOR MAN...

Each dawning day brings a new far-out proclamation from the leader of the free world. So it shouldn't have come as a shock when President Trump announced, via Twitter, that he'd be implementing a sixth branch of the U.S. Armed Forces: the Space Force. He reasoned that we have forces for land, air, and sea...so why not the stars? Perplexed members of the Air Force and NASA were about to explain why this wasn't necessary, but it was too late: Trump and Vice President Pence announced that the Space Force would be active by 2020. We can only imagine who might be signing up...

LOOK OUT!

They couldn't pass the physical exams for any other branches of the military.

But that's no problem.

Because they're taking all comers...

SPACE FORCED

TO BOLDLY GO...WHERE NO ONE IS ACTUALLY NEEDED

WRITER **BROCKTON MCKINNEY**   ARTIST **SAM SISCO**

A TV AD WE'LL SOON SEE

WRITER: CHRISTIAN ALSIS
ARTIST: ALEJANDRO RIVAS

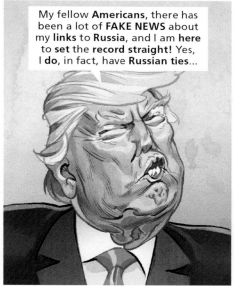

My fellow **Americans**, there has been a lot of **FAKE NEWS** about my **links** to Russia, and I am **here** to **set** the **record straight!** Yes, I **do**, in fact, have **Russian ties**...

Introducing *Donald Trump's Russian Ties*, **American-made,** Russia-themed ties from **Trump International!**

[*Made in American-owned factories in China]

Whether you're **working tirelessly** for the **American people**...

Having **GREAT** meetings, the **BEST** meetings, with other **world leaders**...

Spending **downtime** at **home** with your **family**...

Or **posing** for your official Presidential portrait...

Trump's Russian Ties are **guaranteed** to **Make American Necks Great Again!**™

TRUMP'S RUSSIAN TIES
Interfering in your wardrobe this season. You'll find a bigly variety at your local **Peter the Great-Priced Clothing Superstore** today!

103

WRITER & ARTIST **TERESA BURNS PARKHURST**

QUESTIONS WE'D LIKE TO ASK DONALD TRUMP

WRITER **BARRY LIEBMANN**   ARTIST **RICK TULKA**

SEEN ON TRUMP'S COMPUTER

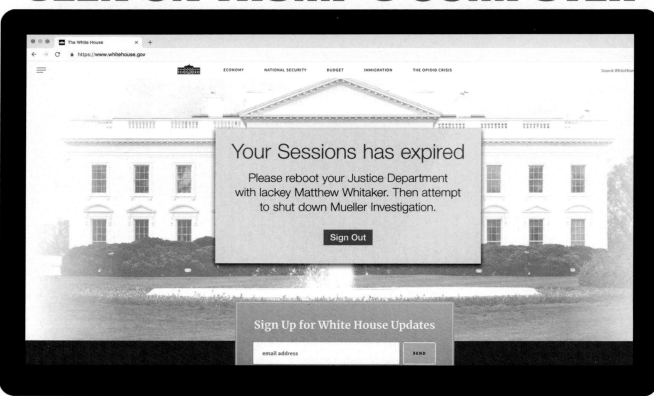

BILL AND KATHY'S TASTELESS JOKES
FROM JEST TO WORST

When it comes to making jokes that miss the mark, offend many and totally bomb, no one beats MAD! Even so, we'd be remiss in our duty if we didn't give a squeeze of the old rubber chicken to Kathy Griffin and Bill Maher. In May, Griffin posted a photo of herself holding a bloodied, severed-head mask of Donald Trump, quickly apologized for it, and later apologized for her apology. A few weeks later, Maher, during an interview, casually referred to himself as a "house n***er," brushed it off as no big deal, and later apologized for doing "a bad thing." Not since Ethel and Julius Rosenberg (Look them up!) has America been so shocked by a couple. Maybe they should team up and take their act on the road.

HBO AND CNN PRESENT...

Tone-Deaf COMEDY Jam

Bill Maher
"Work in the fields? I'm a house n***er."

Kathy Griffin
"I caption this 'there was blood coming out of his eyes, blood coming out of his...wherever.'"

WARNING: DUE TO CLASSLESS, INDEFENSIBLE "JOKES," VIEWER ENJOYMENT IS IMPOSSIBLE

"There is no reason for these massive, deadly, and costly fires except that management is so poor."

"Don't worry, it's just a temporary ban until we can figure out what is going on."

WRITER & ARTIST **LARS KENSETH**

CHRIS CHRISTIE CLOSES JERSEY BEACHES
THAR HE BLOWS!

After eight years of bluster and bullying—not to mention the Bridgegate scandal and a doomed Presidential bid—New Jersey residents have learned that Governor Chris Christie is the kind of guy they wouldn't want to hang out with, even if it was on a vast expanse of beach. Well, that's something they didn't have to worry about last Fourth of July weekend, when, citing a budget impasse, Christie ordered the state's beaches closed—then got caught red-handed (no doubt from sun exposure) relaxing with his family on one of the very beaches he'd just shut down! It's clear that Christie no longer gives a s#!t about what his constituents think of him. Maybe what he needs is a long vacation, far away from the voters he's screwed and alienated during his failed administration.

Exhausted from defending your indefensible actions? Take a break at...

Scandals

Enjoy the kind of privacy you can only get from closing down all state beaches!

Soak up heat you haven't experienced since the early days of Bridgegate!

Feel your stress level drop faster than your approval rating!

Scandals

BECAUSE YOU'RE A LAME DUCK, AND YOU DON'T GIVE A F**K!

ABUSE YOUR POWER WHILE YOU CAN! BOOK NOW!

ARTIST: ROBERTO PARADA

Given the *New York Times* article claiming Trump isn't a self-made billionaire, here's...

OTHER THINGS THAT WEREN'T SELF-MADE BY DONALD TRUMP

A HAM SANDWICH

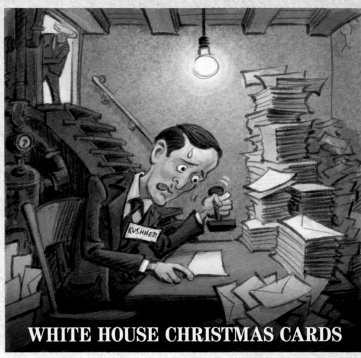

WHITE HOUSE CHRISTMAS CARDS

THE LEFT TURN INTO MCDONALD'S DRIVE-THRU

NAFTA

What's on Michael Cohen's 100 Tapes

20% What Melania calls 'Boy's Talk' (or what everyone else calls objectifying women)

16% Either Trump firing Cohen or Cohen begging for his job back

4% Pillow talk with Sean Hannity

7% Prank calls to Obama or Hillary

8% Pleading phone calls with Putin, re: pee tape

2% Actual business

12% Five rare Prince studio cuts

8% Arguing over pizza toppings

9% Knock-knock jokes

14% Ordering pizza

WRITER & ARTIST **BOB ECKSTEIN**

Trump responds to dismissal of Stormy Daniels' lawsuit.

WHITE HOUSE STAFF FIRINGS S#!T, CANNED

When he was campaigning, Donald Trump said that he would only hire "the best people." If by "best people" he meant "bungling treasonists," then he succeeded quite well—although they sure didn't stick around for long! In less than a year, Trump showed the door to a half-dozen of his "best" people. We're sensing a trend—and we can only hope that when Trump runs out of people to fire, he'll take a look in the mirror, throw up in his mouth a little and give *himself* the axe.

EVERYTHING IS *NOT* AWESOME AT 1600 PENNSYLVANIA AVENUE!

DONALD TRUMP

IN

THE LET GO MOVIE

THEY'RE FIRED!

STARRING
MIKE FLYNN   REINCE PRIEBUS   STEVE BANNON *and* ANTHONY SCARAMUCCI
IN A BRIEF CAMEO ROLE

ARTIST: DEAN MACADAM

DETENTION CENTERS PUT CHILDREN IN CAGES MISERY FOR ALL AGES

President Trump's "zero tolerance" immigration policy promised to prosecute all who illegally entered the United States, including asylum-seekers. By June, thousands of kids had been separated from their parents along the U.S.-Mexico border, with children being held in cages described as "freezing cold," "without access to adequate bathroom facilities," and "thoroughly inhumane." Trump would eventually reverse the policy—but with seemingly no plan in place to reunite families, many kids are still on their own (and may never be reunited)! We can only imagine how some heartless businessman could profit from this obscene attack on human rights with a new board game the whole/separated family can enjoy...

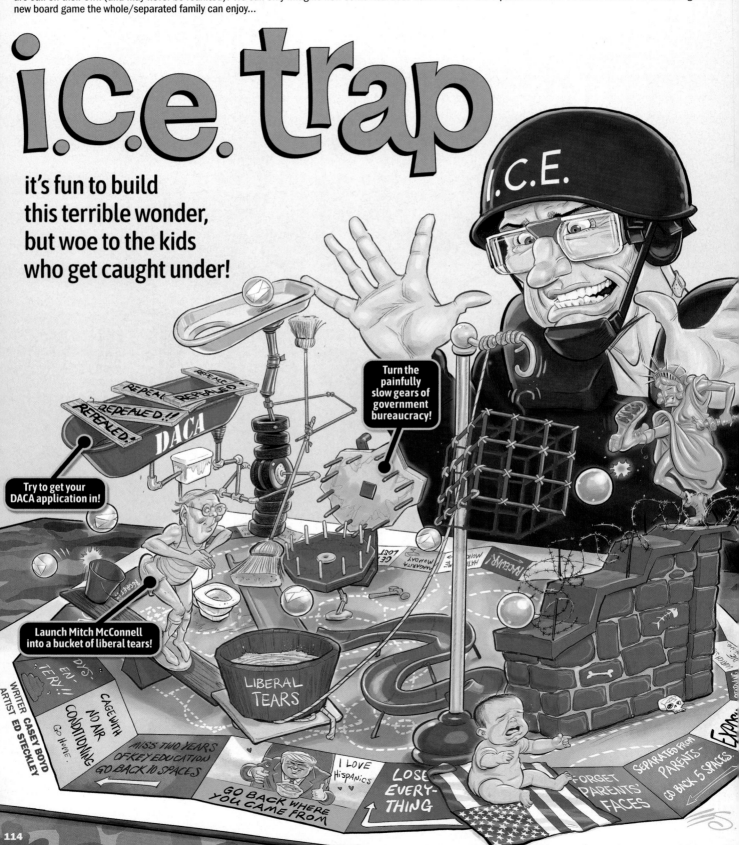

WHAT SEISMIC SHIFTS ARE FRIGHTENING MANY AMERICANS?

HERE WE GO WITH ANOTHER RIDICULOUS
MAD FOLD-IN

There's something just under the surface that was untapped for years, but is now being brought out in the worst ways possible. The devastating result is damaging our country, yet there's no sign that it will stop. To find out what this horrifying shake-up is, fold page in as shown.

FOLD PAGE OVER LIKE THIS!

A   FOLD PAGE OVER LEFT   B FOLD BACK SO THAT "A" MEETS "B"

EARTH-SHAKING PROTESTS ARE EVERYWHERE NOW. INEQUALITY PLAYS A BIG PART. CORRECTING IT ALL TAKES CAREFUL SHARING OF TAX MONEY WITH PEOPLE ABUSED BY FREQUENT HARDSHIP. FAIR PLAY, SADLY, IS STILL LACKING

A   WRITER AND ARTIST: AL JAFFEE   B

Want to spare this precious page for posterity? Turn to page 128 to see the resolved Fold-In

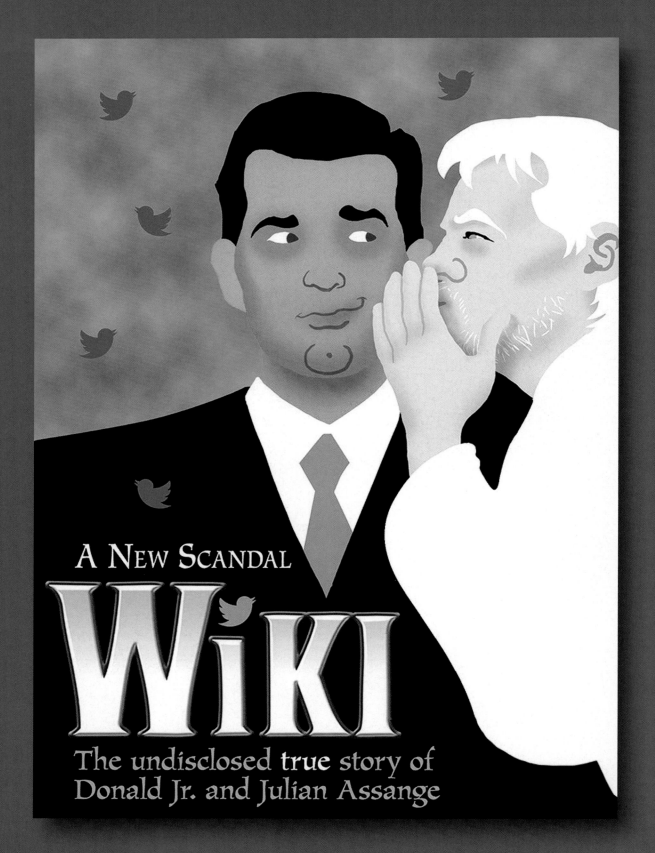

"Heads up, sir. Merlin has written a tell-all parchment."

WRITERS **SCOTT DOOLEY & JASON CHATFIELD**   ARTIST **JASON CHATFIELD**

6 REASONS WHY OMAROSA LEFT THE WHITE HOUSE

Trump decided that the White House was only big enough for ONE abrasive, dangerously unqualified reality-TV hack

She's decided to move on to other made-up positions that don't actually exist

Trump will need her office for lawyers once impeachment hearings start

With the holidays approaching, she needed to focus on her duties as Krampus

She wanted to spend more time with the remaining family members she hadn't ostracized

There was simply nothing left for her to achieve

A SURPRISE SPEECH FROM CHARLTON HESTON

WRITER **CASEY BOYD**   ARTIST **LUKE MCGARRY**

TRUMP'S RESPONSE TO PUERTO RICO
THROWING IN THE TOWELS

Did you know that Puerto Rico is an American commonwealth whose residents are United States citizens? Many Americans were reminded of these facts and rushed to help after Hurricane Maria devastated the island in September. Which is more than we can say for President Trump, who acted as if the catastrophe happened in some obscure foreign land. A week after Maria left thousands without food or water, Trump finally got off his flabby ass, flew down, tossed around some Brawny and got the hell out of there. Of course, he saved most of his Puerto Rico-related energy for—what else?—a petty Twitter war with San Juan's exasperated mayor. With his crudeness, moral corruption and lack of empathy, we'd compare Trump to a pirate—but that would be an insult to pirates.

"I hate to tell you... but you've thrown our budget a little out of whack because we've spent a lot of money on Puerto Rico."

"We now actually have military distributing food—something that, really, they shouldn't have to be doing."

"We cannot keep FEMA, the Military & the First Responders... in P.R. forever!"

"They [Puerto Ricans] want everything done for them when it should be a community effort."

DONALD TRUMP PRESENTS
TYRANT of the CARIBBEAN
BRINGING PAPER TOWELS TO PUERTO RICO

ARTIST: ALEJANDRO RIVAS

"Just imagine you're Brett Kavanaugh's reputation!"

WRITER & ARTIST **LARS KENSETH**

WRITER **DAN TELFER**   ARTIST **LUKE MCGARRY**

DR. CHRISTINE BLASEY FORD EXPLAINS HOW OTHER THINGS WORK TO CONGRESS

ARTIST **GIDEON KENDALL**

WHAT IS THIS YEAR'S BIGGEST NEWS STORY?

HERE WE GO WITH ANOTHER RIDICULOUS
MAD FOLD-IN

There's been a tremendous amount of coverage of the Trump administration, but there's one story so huge, it's unreal! The reports are absolutely incredible and they won't go away. To find out what unbelievable story is dominating the news, fold page in as shown.

FOLD PAGE OVER LIKE THIS!

▲ A

FOLD PAGE OVER LEFT ◄ B FOLD BACK SO THAT "A" MEETS "B"

In the classic and twisted ABC book *The Gashlycrumb Tinies*, illustrator Edward Gorey famously killed off 26 children in alphabetical order—one death for each letter. Each unfortunate event was as different as it was gothic—the characters were dispatched by every method imaginable, including bears, trains, and falling statues.

Sadly, times have changed and there's basically one way that most kids seem to die now. With that in mind, we solemnly present...

THE GHASTLYGUN TINIES

WRITER **MATT COHEN**   ARTIST **MARC PALM**

A is for ALICE the young science wiz

B is for BRIAN cramming for a quiz

C is for CONNOR in his English class

D is for DANA who had a hall pass

E is for EVE who's idealistic

F is for FRANK, more than a statistic

G is for GREG who was caught unawares

H is for HIRO who needs more than prayers

I is for IKE learning Shakespeare by rote

J is for JULIE who's too young to vote

K is for KARA who's weary today

L is for LIAM reading Hemingway

M is for MEGAN who's studying math

N is for NATHAN who's caught in the path

O is for OWEN learning about states

P is for PAULA protecting classmates

Q is for QUINN whose life had just begun

R is for REID, valued less than a gun

S is for STEPHEN who's planning for prom

T is for TINA who's texting her mom

U is for UNA who ID'ed his face

V is for VINCENT who's sheltered in place

W is for WENDY, kind beyond belief

X is for XENA whose dad's crushed by grief

Y is for YURI whose time has now passed

Z is for ZOE who won't be the last

WHAT IS THIS YEAR'S BIGGEST NEWS STORY?

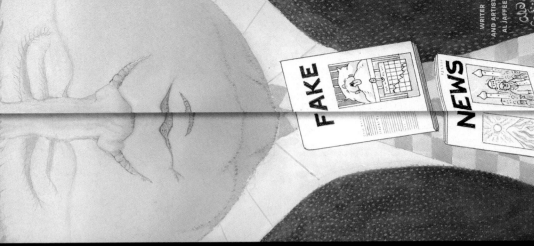

FAKE NEWS

WHAT SEISMIC SHIFTS ARE FRIGHTENING MANY AMERICANS?

EARTH-QUAKES CAUSED BY FRACKING

WHAT ENDLESS WARS HAS THE TRUMP ADMINISTRATION INEXPLICABLY SUPPORTED?

ALEX JONES INFO WARS

FOLD PAGE OVER LIKE THIS!

A B FOLD BACK SO THAT "A" MEETS "B"